# The Romantic Tradition
# in American Literature

# The Romantic Tradition in American Literature

*Advisory Editor*

HAROLD BLOOM
Professor of English, Yale University

# POEMS,

ORIGINAL AND TRANSLATED,

BY

# CHARLES T. BROOKS

SELECTED AND EDITED

By W. P. ANDREWS

ARNO PRESS

A NEW YORK TIMES COMPANY

New York • 1972

**Reprint** Edition 1972 by Arno Press Inc.

Reprinted from a copy in The Wesleyan
University Library

The Romantic Tradition in American Literature
ISBN for complete set: 0-405-04620-0
See last pages of this volume for titles.

Manufactured in the United States of America

☙ॐॐॐॐॐॐॐॐॐ

**Library of Congress Cataloging in Publication Data**

Brooks, Charles Timothy, 1813-1883.
    Poems, original and translated.

    (The Romantic tradition in American literature)
    On spine:  Poems and memoir.
    I.  Series.
PS1123.B83P7  1972        811'.3      72-4952
ISBN 0-405-04624-3

# POEMS,

*ORIGINAL AND TRANSLATED,*

BY

# CHARLES T. BROOKS.

With a Memoir.

# POEMS,

## ORIGINAL AND TRANSLATED,

BY

# CHARLES T. BROOKS.

WITH

## 𝔄 𝔐emoir

BY CHARLES W. WENDTE.

SELECTED AND EDITED

BY W. P. ANDREWS.

BOSTON:
ROBERTS BROTHERS.
1885.

𝔘niversity 𝔓ress:
JOHN WILSON AND SON, CAMBRIDGE.

## CHARLES T. BROOKS.

Dear Poet Soul! whose gentle, tuneful lyre
Has soothed with music many another's woe;
How shall we sing of thee, now, sweet and low,
Thou hear'st thy welcome from the perfect choir?
How shall we sing of thee? Our loves aspire
To voice thy worth, that all the world may know;
The full heart falters: ah! no more! — but so —
And fond words die as deepens our desire.

"Half Lamb, half Cowper!" All thy pure heart's
    strings
Trembled in music with the breath of heaven;
And like a quiet brook that laughs and sings,
Thy glad life glided from clear pools, above
And in whose mirrored deeps bright stars of even
Smiled a still benison of peace and love.

                                  *W. P. A.*

*Not by literature or theology, but only by rare integrity, by a man permeated and perfumed with airs of Heaven,— with manliest or womanliest enduring love,— can the vision be clear.*

EMERSON.

# EDITORIAL NOTE.

———◆———

"THOSE who listened to Lord Chatham felt that there was something finer in the man than in anything which he said," writes Emerson. And when Mr. Brooks's friend Mr. E. A. Silsbee says of him: "He was half Lamb, half Cowper,— but in genius of temperament rather than in his work," one feels alike the force of the statement and its qualification. Yet something of his earnest spirituality and of the delightful, sympathetic humor that lightly played over the deeper waves of his thought and feeling are mirrored in the softly-flowing measures of Mr. Brooks's verse; though to his intimate friends, at least, it can never quite reflect the charm of his gracious personality.

Graceful, pure, and sweet, full of poetic fancies, his song is always; and often fulfils Wordsworth's definition of "all good poetry," — "the spontaneous overflow of feeling." This makes the value of the poetry here selected, which will favorably compare with the verse of his admired contemporaries. If this may not be as confidently asserted of his " occasional" compositions, dependent, rather, upon the determination of his will, their harmonious cadences have consoled and uplifted many a sorrowing heart, and brightened many a serious or gay assembly. " Composition so produced," however, says Shelley, " is to poetry what mosaic is to painting." Our poet, unfortunately, has heretofore been more generally known by his verse of this character; and hence the true value of his poetical work has not always been adequately estimated.

It is to be regretted that the plan and limits of this volume, the first formal publication of his original poetry, could not allow the admission of more of Mr. Brooks's delicate and especially characteristic drolleries. Enough, however, is given to indicate this side of his genial nature, which here also shows itself in his translations. These last have been chosen with a view to illustrate his varied ability in this field of literary work, where he was singularly successful; his graceful and very faithful renderings of the poetry of other languages having always an idiomatic English dress. This is perhaps nowhere more apparent than in his rendering of

Uhland's lines " On the Death of a Country Pastor," which he applied to the memory of his friend and brother poet, the late Jones Very, of his native town. Not less applicable are they to his own gentle spirit, whose outward semblance recalled alike the poet and the Fatherland that gave these verses birth ; and with them we close the volume.

WILLIAM P. ANDREWS.

Salem, Mass., April, 1885.

# CONTENTS.

———◆———

## Translations.

# MEMOIR.

# MEMOIR.

Charles Timothy Brooks was born in Salem,
Mass., on Sunday, June 20, 1813, the second child
of Timothy and Mary King (Mason) Brooks. His
earliest ancestor on this side the water was one
Henry Brooks, whose name appears on the tax lists
of Woburn, Mass., in 1649, and as a selectman of
that town in later years. There the family lived
through five successive generations. Timothy Brooks,
born in Woburn in 1751, moved to Salem in 1777 or
1778, where his son, the fourth Timothy, was born,
Oct. 2, 1786. He was the father of the poet, who
is therefore of the eighth generation from his Puri-
tan ancestor. He seems to have inherited from his
father, in part at least, his amiable disposition; and
from both sides of his family his artistic and literary
proclivities. His mother was descended from the
eminent Puritan divine, the Rev. Francis Higginson,
who was born in England in 1587, and died at Salem
in 1630. It is always difficult to trace characteristics
of disposition to individual ancestors; but the ster-
ling moral qualities, the refinement of feeling, the
responsive reverence of mind which were noted in

Mr. Brooks, even in early youth, were the natural outcome of his lineage and early surroundings.

For the first fifteen years of his life the boy remained in his father's house, attending meanwhile various elementary schools. For several years he was a pupil of his maternal aunt, Miss Abigail Mason,— a cultivated, bright, and witty woman, with whom in after life he maintained affectionate relations, and who exerted no little influence for good upon his development. In 1824, at the age of eleven, he entered the Latin Grammar School in Salem, at which he completed his preparation for college. Henry K. Oliver, Esq., of Salem, who was usher in the Latin School when Charles Brooks entered it, and who survives his pupil in a beautiful and honored old age, thus writes of the boy : —

" My love for him was a love at first sight. I most distinctly remember his slight figure, his calm and attractive face, and his quiet and gentle way and manner. The boy was father to the man, and we became — what is too infrequent between teacher and scholar — intimate friends, our friendship enduring through life. He was literally a faultless boy, winning the love of masters and associates without effort, by the mere unaffected action of his inborn nature and disposition. Never was even mildest reproof, by either word or look or hint, called out by him ; and yet he was active, lively, and of constant, unvarying good-humor, playful with his mates in playtime, and earnest and studious in study-time. So native to him was it to be and to do right that he was and he did right unconsciously, without effort, at all times and under all circumstances, his innate ingenuousness banishing all affectation."

This gentle, teachable disposition, quick apprehension, and fondness for study caused him to make rapid progress in the acquirement of knowledge, and he carried off various prizes for pre-eminence in scholarship. But these schoolboy honors were as meekly borne as they were well deserved and gladly accorded. "One of the most pleasing memories of my schooldays," writes one of his class, "is that of a group of boys of the lower forms of the Latin School (myself among them) clustered round the desk of Charlie Brooks before the opening of the school, asking of him a solution of our difficulties in translating and scanning Latin verse, in which we were then novices. I well remember his bright and cheery look, the rosy spots in his cheeks, and the ready, willing way in which he solved our difficulties, some of which were the result of obtuseness and others of laziness. But it made no difference to him; he helped us all the same, with no sign of impatience. We regarded him as the particular bright scholar of his class. He was the only one whose aid was thus sought, and I think of no other by whom it would have been so cheerfully given."

It must not be imagined, however, that this amiable and studious youth was averse to the boyish pursuits and pastimes appropriate to his age. On the contrary, the glimpses we obtain of his early years, as they have been so lovingly chronicled by his friend the Rev. E. B. Willson, in a paper [1] on the Salem life

[1] Printed, with other contributions of friends and a genealogy of the Brooks family, in the Historical Collections of the Essex Institute.

of Charles T. Brooks, read before the Essex Institute
of that city, disclose to us a ruddy-cheeked lad —
"Little Blushing" was the nickname given him by
the girls — with cheerful blue eyes, a fine flow of
spirits, and a keen zest for the plays and sports of
boyhood.  His delicate physique forbade any large
participation in the more boisterous games of his
playmates, yet he entered into their spirit, and de-
lighted at this period in books of adventure and
war.  He was already noted for his keen sense of
the ludicrous, and powers of lively repartee.  His
strong love of Nature early manifested itself.  He
would roam for hours and days among the woods and
pastures or along the rock-bound, pebbly-beached
coast of his native town, exquisitely sensitive to
the beauty of sky and earth and sea.  Here, too,
he acquired his taste for fishing, which comported
so well with his Nature-loving, peaceful disposi-
tion, and for which he was afterward renowned at
Newport.

Another great formative influence was the impres-
sion produced on the mind of the growing boy by the
social and business life of his native city.  Salem at
the beginning of the present century was in many
respects one of the most prosperous and remarkable
towns in New England.  A considerable trade with
the East Indies and other parts of the globe imparted
a stir to its streets, and unusual mental activity
to its citizens.  The possession of wealth induced
comfort and elegance in their ways of living, while
intercourse with far distant peoples and large busi-

ness relations fostered a certain breadth of view, vigor, and love of culture for which Salem has ever been noted. There was much that was quaint and eccentric, as well as dignified and courtly, in the looks and bearing of some of its marked and independent old worthies half a century ago, which could not have escaped the keen perceptive faculties and quick humor of the boy; while for all that was venerable and romantic in the historical associations and local traditions of his native town he had through life the utmost reverence and affection.

Stress should be laid also upon the religious influences which were brought to bear upon his youth, and to which he proved peculiarly responsive. It was a period of spiritual awakening and revision of beliefs in New England. The rigors of the Puritan creed were being sensibly softened and the religious horizon widened through a larger contact with the world and an increased culture. The old Calvinistic dogmas were more mildly preached or allowed to lapse altogether, while increased emphasis was laid on the ethical side of piety. The Arminian and Unitarian heresies found congenial soil in the intelligent and cultivated circles of Salem. The parents of young Brooks, who sympathized with the new departure in theology, attended the Old North Church; and no reminiscences of his childhood had a deeper hold than those which were associated with this sacred spot. The words in which the Rev. Mr. Willson, the present pastor of the church, records this impression, may fitly be quoted here : —

" All that belongs to the church scenery made a lasting
impression on his imagination.    The venerable figure of
Dr. Holyoke, the centenarian, standing in the pulpit by the
minister's side through the delivery of the sermon, on
account of his deafness ; the placing of the many notable
persons whom he saw in that congregation as they were to
be seen, say, during the pastorate of Dr. Brazer, in the old
first-built meeting-house ; the reverential, not to say awful
investiture of sanctity with which an imaginative child saw
all the offices of religion clothed, — these things all could
not have failed to hold the attention and stamp the charac-
ter of a sensitive child ; and they may be taken as certified
and important among the factors which gave to Charles
Brooks's mind, even in early childhood, a direction towards
the profession so easily selected when he reached the re-
sponsibilities of young manhood.    Born before the close of
the ministry of Dr. Barnard, the first minister of the church ;
baptized by Mr. Abbot, its youthful saint ; listening with
his quick intelligence, at the most susceptible period of life,
— that is, from the age of eight years to that of fifteen, — and
frequently after, on his vacation and other visits home from
college, to Rev. John Brazer, one of the most scholarly
and able of the men who have maintained the reputation
of the Salem pulpit in the past, and who was even more
distinguished for carrying truth home to conviction, by
close and direct address to the conscience, than for accurate
learning and logical argumentation, acknowledged as was
his high ability in these forms of power, — Charles Brooks
breathed from his earliest childhood the atmosphere, not
only of Salem's best literary and scientific culture, but of
its deepest religious life."

Thus in the tender atmosphere of a well-ordered
and happy home, whose serious ideals of duty were

tempered with the mutual love of parents and chil-
dren, amid stimulating and congenial studies, and
the formative influences of the social and religious
life of his native town, Charles Brooks fulfilled
the divine mission of childhood, growing daily in
wisdom and stature and in favor with God and
man.

In 1828 the youth of fifteen entered Harvard Uni-
versity. Among his classmates were Henry W. Bel-
lows, George Ticknor Curtis, John S. Dwight, John
Holmes, Estes Howe, Samuel Osgood, John Park-
man, William Silsbee, Henry Wheatland, and Augus-
tus Story. Other college mates were Charles Sumner,
J. Lothrop Motley, and Oliver Wendell Holmes. We
are fortunate in possessing quite full memorials of a
part of his college days in the form of a journal kept
during his junior and senior years. A pleasant pic-
ture it gives of the student life at Cambridge half a
century ago. Young Brooks seems to have engaged
in the work of securing a higher education with great
seriousness and ardor. The list of his studies and
literary appointments is truly formidable for one of
his slender strength. He attended eight lectures and
twenty-five recitations a week, besides forensics, de-
bates, and society meetings. His partiality for lin-
guistic studies at once manifested itself. Besides the
classics, in which he pursued the appointed course
under the able guidance of Professors Popkin, Wil-
lard, and Felton, we find him acquiring the French
and Spanish languages under Professor Sales ; and he
is one of a forlorn hope who, at the latter's sugges-

tion, take up Portuguese also. He is deeply inter-
ested in the lectures of Prof. George Ticknor on the
literature of these nations. But more than all else
he enjoys the study of the German tongue, with
whose masterpieces in prose and poetry his name was
to be so honorably identified in after years as trans-
lator and critic. This was largely due, no doubt, to
his rare good fortune in being initiated into the lan-
guage and its literature by those enthusiastic and
eminent German scholars, Dr. Karl Follen and Prof.
Charles Beck. His English studies seem to have
been much helped by the instructions of Prof. E. T.
Channing and the custom of writing frequent foren-
sics, although he confesses that he "toiled terribly"
over the latter. To these numerous engagements
he now added, in order to increase his financial
resources, the duties of a monitor. Under the
former system of paternal college government this
position was an onerous and trying one, and par-
ticularly irksome to his gentle and genial nature.
Once, at least, he seems to have failed in enforcing
the prescribed discipline, and is sent for by President
Quincy, who with some asperity reproves him be-
cause of the scandalous conduct of the students at
prayers. It seems they had acted with great inde-
cency, rushing out of the chapel before the exer-
cises were concluded, and creating much disturbance.
Poor Brooks bears the reproof meekly, although he
is greatly mortified, and at heart thinks the President
unjust towards the monitors. He is somewhat en-
couraged, however, a day or two later, at receiving

unexpected and warm praise from the same source for his work in English composition.

It is not surprising that with such a multiplicity of duties and constant over-application to his studies, his health, always delicate, should begin to suffer. His journal becomes largely a chronicle of aches and ailments. His digestion is disordered, his eyes begin to give him trouble, he is the victim of bad dreams at night, and dulness, languor, and morbid, depressed feelings during the day. For relief he turns with increased zest to physical exercise, for which the opportunities and aids were not in that day as complete in American colleges as now. He takes a daily swim in the Charles River, and goes off on long strolls about Cambridge and its vicinity. Sometimes, he tells us, a little company of students would take their tin pails and go off together on a berrying excursion " in the buryin' ground." One wonders what the Harvard seniors of to-day would say to such Arcadian simplicity of custom. Again he walks to Boston, and runs about the city, visiting its sights, attending the few amusements of those days, calling on friends, and not insensible to the witchery of certain bright eyes, always a magnetic attraction for the Harvard student. Most frequently, however, we find him poring over the treasures of the book-stall, and his diary records the severe struggles he had with himself to limit his purchases by his slender means.

His two annual vacations were usually spent at home in Salem. He thought nothing of making the journey thither on foot, but sometimes the coach was preferred. The stage-driver's stentorian voice awakens him at four o'clock, summoning the passengers to leave their beds. With a dozen other students he crowds into the already well-filled coach. With much squeezing and shaking and laughing and groaning, the party speed their way over the bad roads, arriving at Salem after a rough ride of three and a half hours. His holidays at home were spent in needed rest, visiting friends, or roaming about the fields and woods, fishing-rod in hand, and, we may be sure also, a book in his pocket. Once at least this routine was pleasantly broken by an excursion with a college mate in the summer of 1831 to Eastport, Me., which he keenly enjoyed, and from which he returned with new vigor to his studies. The Italian language was now added; and he speaks also in warm admiration of the lectures of Prof. John Farrar and Drs. J. C. Warren and James Jackson. He also finishes and delivers in public his "much feared" English oration. The topic he has chosen to write on is "Intellectual Independence," which is not without significance as indicating the ideal aims of his youth. It receives some rather severe criticism, especially as regards the manner of its delivery, but on the whole is much liked and commended.

This account of his college life would be very incomplete if it did not present in passing a glimpse of the social life and good fellowship among the students, in which he so greatly delighted, and whose memories were so cherished by him in after years. His journal pictures him sitting among a group of kindred spirits

—Dwight, Story, Dupee, Simmons, Silsbee, Dorr, and others—in his room in old Stoughton. The storm is raging furiously without, and piling snow-drifts about the venerable pile of college buildings. The wind blows so terrifically through the halls and chimneys that it sends the blazing fagots on the hearth scurrying across the room, and forces the very locks off the doors. But above the roar of the storm rises the din of merry voices singing gleeful songs, laughing boisterously at stories for the ninth time repeated, or gayly chaffing each other; while Brooks sits munching his favorite apples, and makes a solemn compact with his friend Appleton not to perpetrate any more bad puns during the remainder of the term,—a resolution he must have found it impossible to keep a single day. Presently the scene changes with the changing seasons. A summer night-breeze gently stirs the old elms on the campus; the moonlight softens the rigid outlines of Holworthy and Stoughton, and silvers their bareness into beauty. Windows are opened wide, and students sit by them dreamily smoking, or lean out to hail a passing mate, or listen to the sweet music raised by the Pierian Sodality, while below in the college yard the Harvard Military Squad is practising its evolutions.

Brooks took much enjoyment also in the Hasty Pudding Club, in which he won his first laurels as poet and orator; but his journal is discreetly silent concerning its secret and mysterious proceedings. He was a faithful attendant at the Society debates, and participated at times in the discussions on the well-worn didactic themes on which successive generations of students have tried the callow wings of their eloquence. He was a great hand, too, for calling on his fellow students, with whom he was a universal favorite; and many were the "social suppers" at which his genial, witty presence was sought. We find him meeting with the Med. Facs. in secret conclave, and anon attending a moot court in Commons hall, presided over by Judge Story, with Seniors as counsel and a jury of solemn Divinity students.

Meanwhile his inclination for linguistic and literary studies discloses itself more and more. He grows enthusiastic over Shakspeare, and reads Plutarch, Gibbon, and among the poets Cowper and Byron, with warm appreciation. He mentions "an unknown writer in the 'Edinburgh Review'" (Carlyle) whose contributions especially interest him. With his aunt Abby Mason and a few college friends, he carries on a lively correspondence on literary and related topics. On Aug. 17, 1831, he notes with humorous self-satisfaction that he has made his first original poem, some verses for an album. They are recorded in his journal, but are hardly worth repeating here. It is his "geliebtes Deutsch" from which he derives the most enjoyment, however. He is now deep in Jean Paul, "der einzige." In his last Senior term he begins Goethe's "Faust," and mourns the death of that "universal genius." He tries his skill at translating German ballads, and attends for the first time a concert of German music, and is quite carried away with the new world of harmony it reveals to him.

We soon find him scribbling poetry on every occasion and subject, and acquiring a dangerous facility in rhyme.

In view of his later choice of a vocation we are especially interested in what he says of the religious life of the college and the character of the preaching to which he listened. The Unitarian movement at that day was in the ascendency throughout eastern Massachusetts, and was the dominating religious influence at the University. Dr. Henry Ware, the elder, gave annually courses of lectures on the history and criticism of the New Testament, in which a liberal and spiritual interpretation of the Scriptures was substituted for the literal and dogmatic methods of the older and Orthodox schools. Young Brooks reports concerning the opening lecture of this course : —

"Dr. Ware began with stating the importance of the books both because of the momentous nature of their contents and the fact of their authors being inspired. Then he gave the different views of this inspiration that had been held. Some thought it plenary; others only a general superintendence of the Divine Spirit, leaving all minor matters to each author's taste. But at any rate, we didn't doubt that they were extraordinarily gifted writers, etc."

Among the text-books of the college course were Paley's Evidences and Butler's Analysis, over which he spent weary but not unprofitable hours. A more quickening influence came to him from Prof. E. T. Channing, brother of the great divine, at whose house gathered a little circle of students to discuss the great topics of religion and moral duty. Taylor's discourses, Priestley on miracles, and the Unitarian doctrines as they were formulated half a century ago, furnished the subjects for their inquiry and interchange of opinion.

The preaching of that day was earnest, dignified, and lofty in tone, with an academic purity of diction and elegance of form, but it was often unimpassioned, didactic, and dry. In their reaction against the current Orthodoxy, with its narrow, intense dogmatism on the one hand, and emotional waste on the other, the Unitarian clergy addressed themselves too exclusively to the reason and conscience of their hearers, and but slightly appealed to imagination and feeling. This prevailing type of moral discourse was naturally intensified in the college pulpit by the aspects and needs of student life. Our Senior made a careful abstract of the sermons to which he listened, a custom not unusual among the students at that day. The college preacher, Henry Ware, he seems to have liked exceedingly, but is not always edified with the others whom he heard. Dr. J. G. Palfrey he refers to in warm terms. His discourse was " sound, serious, direct, animating, and strengthening, and especially helpful to me on the subject of the Lord's Supper, about which I am not sure." He notes how little sermons affect the hearers. They are moved by them generally, not individually. "They discuss the preacher, not his discourse." Dr. Lowell, father of the poet, and pastor at the West Church, Boston, preached one of his fifteen minutes'

homilies. "Simple, eloquent, direct, and touching,"
reports his young hearer. "I was more impressed
by it than by six or eight ordinary discourses. He
used the emphatic pause with great effect, seeming
to challenge an answer." Of Dr. Ezra S. Gannett,
Channing's colleague, he says, "I liked the man
better than the manner." What would the Doctor
have said to that? In Boston he goes to the Bethel
to hear the eloquent preacher to the sailors, Father
Taylor. "Astonishing! how he careers over the
whole surface and yet sounds as he goes. I never
knew the might of words so till I heard him."

Of the sermon of the great New York divine,
Dr. Dewey, he gives a careful abstract, but makes
no comment. On the 17th of April, 1831, he hears
in Dr. Brazer's pulpit at Salem the young preacher
of the Second Church, Boston, — the Rev. Ralph
Waldo Emerson. "His sermon was characterized by
an earnest, calm eloquence. His text was, 'For we
must all appear before the judgment-seat of Christ,'
which he makes out to be the Christian religion,
whose principles ever condemn the wrong-doer."

We mark a growing seriousness in the tone of his
journal. His literary tastes, moral ideals, and in-
born reverence were already leading him to think
of the ministry as his future vocation. He in-
dulges more in devout reflections. "That virtue
and moral energy which I have so dwelt upon in
the abstract, may I practise for my own and others'
good; that religion whose cause by form I have
espoused, may I adorn and promote by character

2

and conduct." These words seem to have been written on the occasion of his becoming a member of the University Church of Harvard College, on May 26, 1832.

The remaining months sped rapidly away, and his graduation was close at hand. Edward Everett came to examine the Senior Class, and looked "terribly bored." Afterward he came again to deliver the Phi Beta Kappa Oration before a distinguished assembly of literary men. Charles Brooks was vividly reminded that his college years were over, and the serious work of life begun, when Professor Felton sent for him and made him a flattering proposal to remain with him as Greek tutor and proctor. His decision, however, was already made in favor of the ministerial profession, — a choice with which his parents also were heartily agreed. It was his desire to spend a year in teaching school before he entered upon his theological studies. Accordingly letters were written to various parties, in the hope of securing a suitable situation. In this, however, he was unsuccessful. President Quincy proposed to him to enter at once on graduation the Divinity School of Harvard College; but Charles Brooks had scruples, which were to his credit, about being any longer a burthen to his father in the matter of support. While he still hesitated, a gentleman in Salem, — Mr. S. C. Phillips, — who took great interest in the pure-minded and promising youth, and who was devotedly attached to the Liberal Christian movement, generously offered to defray the necessary expenses of his theological course, and urged his acceptance in an admirable letter. To such noble insistence and his parents' counsel, Charles Brooks could but yield, although still with some hesitation. He deeply felt the greatness of the minister's vocation, and his own inadequacy for its duties and requirements.

His journal closes with a few pleasant allusions to the stirring experiences of Commencement Day, — the Governor in his carriage, surrounded by his showy staff; the glittering troop of light horse; the merry crowds on the campus ; the students in their gowns ; the young ladies in their finery; the music; the spreads; the festivities and games, — that celebrated the departure from Alma Mater of another company of well-trained and well-disposed youth to enter upon the serious business of life.

A young lady friend from Salem, who was present, wrote home under date of Aug. 30, 1832 : —

"Yesterday was Commencement. Charles Brooks graduated. I felt highly honored to be one of the number invited by him to Cambridge. He had one of the first pieces for his part. I am told that Charles is very much esteemed at Cambridge, am very glad of it, and should think his friends had reason to be proud of him. . . . There were about forty of us to dine in Charles's room. His tables were set in such a way that the taste of the eye was as much gratified as that of the mouth. . . . The performances of the young men were all very good, — some, I should think, of a high order. Charles's I shall try and get to copy. It was serious, rather. He intends to be a minister. The day was charming."

These pleasant reminiscences of his college days, which we have gleaned from his journals, make us regret the more the absence of any such memoranda concerning the three years passed at the Divinity School in Cambridge. We can therefore dwell but briefly on this interesting and important period in his life.

At the time Charles Brooks entered upon his theological studies, the Unitarian movement in New England had passed from an intellectual and moral protest to an ecclesiastical organization. The stormy controversies it had awakened were dying out; its struggle for recognition was over. The new sect was well established, and included a large proportion of the literary culture, social prestige, moral worth, and religious earnestness of New England. Over one hundred churches organized prior to the Revolutionary War, including the original Pilgrim Church at Plymouth, united in forming the Unitarian body, while new congregations were springing up throughout the country. The Faculty at Harvard College was overwhelmingly in sympathy with the new departure in theology; and a group of admirable and scholarly men — the Wares (father and son), Prof. Andrews Norton, Prof. J. G. Palfrey, and others — conducted the Cambridge Divinity School in accordance with the principles of free inquiry, a rational method, and a spiritual Christianity. In the same class with Charles Brooks were Cyrus A. Bartol, Samuel Osgood, Christopher P. Cranch, John Parkman, and John S. Dwight. Other

fellow-students at the school were George E. Ellis,
A. A. Livermore, William Silsbee, Theodore Parker,
Henry W. Bellows, E. H. Sears, and R. P. Stebbins.

There were some thirty students in all, — a sin-
gularly gifted and spiritually-minded band of youth,
whose daily companionship, even more than the per-
sonal weight and able instructions of the Faculty,
must have inspired our young theologian. A lead-
ing feature in the first year's course were the
lectures of Dr. Henry Ware, Sr., on the "Christian
Evidences." In Systematic Theology he listened to
Prof. Henry Ware, Jr., and to Prof. Andrews Nor-
ton on Sacred Literature. Dr. Convers Francis held
the chair of Homiletics and Pastoral Care ; Prof.
E. T. Channing gave instruction in Sacred Oratory ;
Professor Palfrey was Dean of the Faculty, lectured
on Biblical Archæology and kindred topics, and con-
ducted the daily prayers. At the evening service
one of the Senior Class led in prayer, and every
Sabbath throughout the year the Seniors preached in
turn.

During the last year of the course the study of
Hebrew and New-Testament criticism was added ;
and an afternoon class met for exercise in extem-
poraneous preaching under the guidance of Henry
Ware, Jr. There were also frequent religious meet-
ings held by the students, and a Philanthropic So-
ciety was formed among them for the discussion
of reform and social topics. We can imagine how
entirely the studious, peaceful, and devout atmos-
phere of the Divinity School accorded with the

tastes and ideals of Charles Brooks. He seems to
have found time and strength, amid his new duties,
to undertake the tuition of a pupil, — a boy in Bos-
ton. Above all, we may be sure, his beloved German
was not neglected. Under the direction of Professors
Follen and Beck he continued to read extensively
in the literature of that tongue, — his enthusiasm
for which was shared and stimulated by his fellow-
students, John S. Dwight, Samuel Osgood, Theodore
Parker, C. P. Cranch, and others. On his leaving
college Dr. Follen had certified of him that he was
"thoroughly acquainted with the principles of the
German language, and able to read with precision
and ease the standard German authors." He now
enlarged greatly the range of his acquaintance with
this tongue and its masterpieces, and acquired an
unusual insight into its dialectic structure and
idioms. His facility in rendering into English
rhyme the most difficult forms of German verse was
already noted, and certain of the translations which
later appeared in print were made at this time.

Beside the influences already referred to which
were brought to bear on him at the Cambridge Di-
vinity School, there was another, just making itself
felt in religious and social circles, by which Charles
Brooks and his fellow-students could not be other-
wise than profoundly affected. It was the dawning
of that new movement in religious thought and life
known as Transcendentalism, and which produced so
deep an impression on the ideas and institutions, the
morals, philosophy, and reforms, of New England in

the second third of our century. Transcendentalism
was in New England a reaction against the prevail-
ing realism and sense-philosophy of Locke, Clarke,
and Paley, and the infallibility claimed for Scripture
and tradition. It asserted against these the su-
premacy of the innate ideas and spiritual intuitions
of the human mind, and maintained the paramount
authority of the individual conscience and will.

The new spirit which was soon to agitate profoundly
the religious and especially the Unitarian circles of
New England early made its way into the Divinity
School. In 1832, the year in which Charles Brooks
entered, Ralph Waldo Emerson had laid down his
charge in Boston, and preached that epoch-making
sermon in which he ascribed his resignation to his
scruples about the Communion service, — seemingly
unconscious as yet of the deeper tides that were sweep-
ing him on as the prophet of a new ethical and spir-
itual era. The years that followed witnessed the
gradual and sure advance of the Transcendental faith
in the Unitarian pulpits and pews of eastern Massachu-
setts. Among the little band of ardent youth at the
Divinity School were some who were known not long
afterward as its earnest advocates and leading repre-
sentatives. We may be sure, then, that it was already
a subject of deep interest and lively discussion among
them. The theological faculty, headed by Professors
Ware and Norton, strongly opposed the new move-
ment, as did most of the Unitarian teachers of that
day. Reared in the old schools of theology, they had
no mind to exchange their assured philosophic and

ethical basis for so mystical, unsystematic, and revolutionary a form of belief. Yet there were notable exceptions to this general attitude of the clergy, and certain of the most prominent preachers in and about Cambridge inclined to the new school of thought. It was noted that two of the most eminent of these — Dr. James Walker, later the President of Harvard College, and the Rev. Frederic H. Hedge — early assumed the Transcendental ground. In Watertown Dr. Convers Francis, also a member of the Divinity School faculty, favored it. In Boston, among others the Rev. George Ripley was its earnest defender; while Dr. William E. Channing, although never becoming a partisan in its behalf, soon gave it eloquent expression in his sermons and ethical writings. It does not fall within our province to trace its later history, and show how it gradually became the dominant philosophy of religion in the Unitarian body, which is still largely controlled by it.

But it is certain that the new views greatly influenced Charles Brooks, and shaped more than he was himself aware his theological and ethical opinions. He was indeed a natural Transcendentalist, and could hardly, with his mental constitution and antecedents, have been anything else. This influence is distinctly traceable throughout his later career. It transfused his prayers and discourses, decided his selection of such authors as Goethe, Rückert, Jean Paul, and Schefer for translation, inspired his own verse with spontaneity and fervor, and imparted to him that broad spiritual and forward-looking attitude which, as we shall have opportunity to observe in this memoir, characterized him as a man of literature and a teacher of religion. Later he became an occasional contributor to the "Dial," and in 1838 offered his tribute, a volume of translated German poetry, to the "Specimens of Foreign Standard Literature," edited by George Ripley in the interests of the Transcendental philosophy. Meanwhile his sympathy with the new school of thought was never obtrusive; perhaps it was never thorough and complete. His inborn humility and reverence for past traditions and forms, a certain lack of incisiveness in his mental make-up, and his dislike of all partisanship prevented any such enthusiastic avowal as to some minds, differently constituted, was easy and inevitable.

In the summer of 1835 Charles T. Brooks graduated with honor from the Cambridge Divinity School, his part at Commencement being an English oration, the subject of which has not been preserved.

The years of preparation were now over, and the young minister was ready and eager for the serious work of his profession. For some months he preached in various pulpits, and occasionally as a candidate, wondering meanwhile whither the Providence would finally direct his footsteps and appoint his service. The first sermon entered in his record seems to have been preached at Nahant and elsewhere, and was entitled "The Voice of the Spirit," the text being Hebrews iii. 15: "To-day if ye will hear his voice, harden not your hearts." This choice of a topic would seem to indicate that he had at the outset the spirit of an Evangelist, and felt himself to be the bearer of a divine message to his hearers. We find him occupying the pulpits of Dr. W. E. Channing, Dr. Lowell, Dr. Putnam, and Dr. Parkman in Boston, and of Dr. Dewey in New York. He also preached at Waltham and East Lexington, and at South Scituate, where it was hoped he might be permanently settled as pastor. The winter of 1835–36 he spent with the newly organized society in Augusta, Me. It was the coldest season since 1780, the thermometer on one occasion marking 34° below zero. Conflagrations and business failures increased the prevailing depression; and this, with the rigors of the climate, determined him, though reluctantly, not to accept their cordial invitation to remain with them. The following summer was passed at Windsor, Vt.

In the mean time his attention had been called to a promising movement in the interests of Liberal Christianity at Newport, R. I., which eventually became the scene of his life-long labors and his adopted home.

Newport was the birthplace and early home of William Ellery Channing, and for the last twenty years of his life his summer residence. In character, ability, and eminent services to his fellow-men Dr. Channing was perhaps its most distinguished son. Yet so intense was sectarian bigotry in those days that after he became identified with the Liberal and Unitarian cause he could hardly get permission to speak in any church of his native town. Meanwhile, during the summer months, Dr. Channing gave frequent Sunday evening talks to the farmers from the pulpit of the little Christian Church in Portsmouth, on the island a few miles out of Newport. Many were in the habit of resorting thither from town on such occasions, and these privileges of the summer intensified the longing for the stated preaching of Liberal ideas at home. A noble woman, bearing the apostolic name of St. John, with her honored husband, a retired merchant from Mobile, was especially active in stimulating and giving practical form to this desire. In the autumn of 1835 the Rev. Dr. Charles Briggs, — or "Father Briggs," as he was affectionately called, — the venerable and zealous secretary of the American Unitarian Association, appeared at the ever hospitable door of the St. Johns' in Newport, to explore the field, and, if advisable, to organize a Unitarian society. The next Sunday, and for several week-nights following, he preached at the State House to large congregations. On one of these occasions Dr. Channing, who was present, arose and spoke earnest words of congratulation and encouragement. On the 24th of October a meeting was held at the house of William Ellery, a son of the Rhode Island signer of the Declaration of Independence, and a brother to the mother of Dr. Channing. There were present George Wanton Ellery, another son of the signer, and Deputy Collector of the Port; Samuel St. John; Richard K. Randolph, an eminent lawyer of Virginia;

Josiah C. Shaw; James Hammond, bookseller; Charles Gyles; William V. Taylor, sailing-master of Commodore Perry on Lake Erie; Joseph Joslen, the leading classical teacher in Newport; and Robert J. Taylor. At this and subsequent meetings the society was organized and strengthened by the accession of many of the most liberal and earnest as well as socially prominent of the residents of the town. The old meeting-house in which that doughty Calvinist Dr. Hopkins had preached so unrelentingly the stern decrees of Jehovah, and lifted up his brave, rebuking voice against the national and local sin of slavery, was at this time offered for sale. The new society purchased and remodelled it. A charter was obtained from the Legislature for the " Unitarian Congregational Church of Newport, R. I.," officers were chosen, and regular Sunday services conducted by various ministers from Boston and Providence. The society was now ready and anxious to settle a pastor. After hearing various candidates without coming to a decision, the ever watchful and devoted Father Briggs called the attention of the committee to Charles T. Brooks, and he was invited to preach to the society. But he shall give his own account of his first visit to Newport : —

"On Saturday, May 29, 1836, I came in the steamer 'Massachusetts,' Captain Comstock, from Providence, and set foot for the first time on this island. Landing at Long Wharf, I made my way, with a somewhat vague remembrance of the directions which had been given me, along the grass-grown old pavement of Thames Street as far as

the Custom House, where the image of Benjamin Frank-
lin probably suggested to me to ask my way to the place
of my destination, — Friend Potter's friendly inn ('Quaker
tavern,' some called it), the old original Bellevue House.
'John,' the factotum (still in the bloom of youth in that
capacity at the Ocean House), was disposed at first to doubt
my claim to be the expected 'parson,' but with a droll smile
had to submit.

" On Sunday morning, after a visit to the Beach and a
look down into Purgatory, and an auspicious glance (on my
return) at the sign ' Reading Room ' on the rear of a long,
low building not wholly devoted to that purpose, at the
appointed hour I made my appearance in the quaint place
of our worship, in which the first thing that attracted my
attention was the peculiar, Shaker-like arrangement of the
audience, in seats rising above each other and ranged length-
wise of the hall, the rows of men and women facing each
other on opposite sides of the central aisle ; and the next
was the unusual adornment in the rear of the desk, being —
no crimson curtain nor perspective of sacred columns, but
a relieved work representing a group of musical instru-
ments, rather expressive of a ball-room than of a sanctuary.
In looking back upon my first sermon in that place, I
hardly know which most to marvel at, — the little knowledge
of the demand of occasion and people on my part, in bring-
ing to them so general and abstract a discourse, the subject
being the way of getting and increasing Faith ; or the
little sense on the people's part of what they wanted, shown
by their asking to have the sermon repeated the next Sun-
day evening. However I remember, as if it were yesterday,
the hearty greeting I received after the service. . . . I had
not as yet a presentiment that this was the *Lodge* in life's
*wilderness* which was to be, for so many years to come, my
spiritual and literal home.

"During this first week I passed in Newport, I often visited the work at the church, which was fast approaching completion."

He is described by those who affectionately recall this his first appearance among them, as singularly attractive and winning, slender, with delicate features, and a flush of color in his cheeks which never deserted them even in his old age, making him look, as one has said, "like a pre-Raphaelite saint." The modesty of his demeanor, the simplicity and sweetness of his disposition, the kindly humor which irradiated his conversation, the piety and literary finish of his discourses, so charmed his hearers that there was a quite general desire to secure him as the pastor of the new society. For the time being, however, the young preacher left Newport for desultory service in other pulpits. The old Hopkins meeting-house had in the mean time been prepared for the use of the Unitarian congregation, and on the 27th of July, 1836, was dedicated to Liberal Christian worship, Dr. Channing preaching the sermon, — the famous discourse entitled "The Worship of the Father one of Gratitude and Joy," which is to be found among his published writings.

The impression produced by young Mr. Brooks had not died out, and on the first of August he was invited to return and preach for them again on three Sundays in September. Accordingly he came from Windsor, Vt., where he had been spending the summer, and on the 18th of September preached all day and evening at Newport, but was unable to continue the three Sundays, an attack of stricture of the chest compelling him to return home to Salem for the remainder of the autumn. At the end of December, however, he came back to finish his engagement with the society. "It seems but yesterday," wrote Mr. Brooks many years after, "that the next morning, which was New Year's, while a still snow was falling, I crossed the street, and was greeted by David Carr, who stopped in the midst of sweeping the snow from the steps to touch his hat, with the salutation : ' Are you the parson? I'm the *saxon* of this church.' This quaint introduction and *Right Hand of Fellow-ship* was the pleasant beginning of my ministry in Newport."

A unanimous invitation was now extended him by the new society to become its pastor. This invitation was accepted, and on the 1st of January, 1837, Charles Timothy Brooks entered upon that ministerial relation at Newport which during the thirty-seven years of its continuance so abounded in labors for truth, virtue, and piety, and proved such a blessing for the parish and the larger community. His ordination did not take place till the 14th of June ensuing, when Dr. Brazer of Salem, the pastor of his youth, preached the sermon. The Rev. Drs. F. A. Farley, Edward Hall, and George W. Briggs took part in the services, and Dr. Channing gave the charge. This charge was repeated with slight variations at the ordination of his college classmate, the Rev. John S. Dwight, at Northampton, Mass., a few months later, and is printed among Dr. Channing's works.

"I never shall forget," says Mr. Brooks, "the kindling look of his large luminous eyes, as he turned to me and said, after dwelling on the predominance of 'solemn sound' in the pulpit, 'My brother, help men to see!'"

The field to which the young preacher had been called proved a trying and difficult one. It was, as Mr. Brooks tells us, "a region always historically and locally open to free thought; but there were many elements in the history and habits of the place, and perhaps something in the very elements of its outward nature, enervating to the moral energies, unfavorable to decision of character, unpropitious to earnest, united, and practical thought upon a religion which offers itself to the calm and sober judgment of men as the central motive of the whole life." His early ministry was cast during those exciting and trying times of the great temperance awakening, its violent reaction and relapse, and of the Dorr Rebellion. Throughout all these stirring experiences, he bore firm but gentle witness for the right as it was given him to see the right. It is a testimony to his wise and reconciling ministry, that in the course of time he overcame in large degree this conservative prejudice and sectarian animosity. He maintained amicable and even friendly relations with the other pastors of the city, and exchanged pulpits with Baptist, Methodist, and Presbyterian clergymen. They might not like his doctrines; but they could not but love him, or refrain from paying this tribute to his pure, gentle, and

self-sacrificing ministry. To harmonize the hetero-
geneous ecclesiastical elements composing the newly
formed society, which included come-outers from all
the sects, and sheltered many individual eccentrici-
ties and idiosyncrasies of belief, proved a difficult
task, which only his self-denying and peace-loving
disposition could have successfully accomplished. His
sermons and parish duties in these early years of
his ministry occupied almost his entire thought and
time. It seems to have been believed most de-
voutly at that day that " faith comes by hearing;"
for the preacher was required to hold forth twice and
in winter three times on Sunday, and often a bap-
tism or a funeral service, together with two or three
visits to the sick, rounded out the duties of the day.
This was a severe strain on the slender strength of
the young minister. " I do not forget to this day,"
he writes, in reviewing his earlier pastorate, " the re-
mark of a parishioner, who said in all simplicity, 'I
should think that three sermons was about as much
as a man could write in a week.'" He was also
required to conduct the weekly conference meeting
and the Sunday Bible class, and as a faithful pastor
went from house to house visiting his parishioners,
comforting the sick and sorrowing, inspiring the
faint-hearted, and officiating on all sad and glad
occasions in their lives. It is not surprising that
these excessive labors and cares, together with the
infrequent opportunities for exchange of pulpits, and
the isolation which half a century ago, when the
facilities for travel and intercourse were so much

less than now, was a depressing feature in the island-life of Newport, told seriously against his health and spirits.  He had several severe turns of illness, and would probably have sunk altogether beneath the accumulation of his labors and trials, had it not been for a great blessing which now came to him in the form of a happy marriage and the establishment of a well-ordered home.  On the 18th of October, 1837, he was united in matrimony by Dr. Channing with Miss Harriet Lyman Hazard, the second daughter of Benjamin Hazard, an eminent lawyer and legislator of Newport.  In his wife he secured a true helpmeet and home-keeper, who for the forty-six years of their married life was his loyal, devoted co-worker, and whose energy of character and excellent judgment supplied in large degree those practical elements which were too much wanting in his amiable and unworldly nature.  Life had now begun in earnest for the young preacher, and revealed to him its tenderest side.  With the companionship and affection of his wife and the happy home she made for him, he felt newly strengthened for his work, and faced the exacting duties of his vocation with increased courage and cheerfulness.  His joy was full when, on the 24th day of July, 1838, his first child, Charles Mason Brooks, was born.  A journal kept for a few months after this happy event gives us an interesting insight into the life of the young pastor.  He begins it with an account of the christening of his little son by Dr. Channing, who performed the ceremony " with his wonted simplicity, solemnity, and impressiveness." The journal records further certain of his experiences in visiting among his parishioners. Great stress was laid on the pastor's prayer in the sick-room. Sometimes this was to great mutual edification, but often he complains that his petitions do not come naturally and spontaneously. " Oh, what a wooden prayer ! " he declares, and grows self-accusing and morbid over the perfunctoriness of his religious services. At another time, however, he thankfully acknowledges, "What a living teacher the sick-room is!" His humility did not permit him to realize the power of his childlike and devout personality in the sick-room, or know — what others felt so deeply as they beheld him at prayer — the charm of his rapt, seraphic look, the utter devotion that flushed his cheek, glistened in his eyes, and trembled in his voice. Col. T. W. Higginson relates that once he entered the church while Mr. Brooks was praying. It was a special occasion, and the audience-room was crowded ; so he remained in the vestibule outside. Through the open door he beheld the upturned, adoring face of the preacher. The distance was too great to allow him to distinguish a word of the petition he was uttering ; but the attitude and look of the saintly man, and the cadences of his voice, as they rose and fell, measured, solemn, sweet upon the listening ear, deeply moved his soul to like devotion, and made it one of the most impressive moments which he ever experienced.

On another occasion Mr. Brooks, in visiting the

death-bed of a parishioner, an excellent man, finds
the family much distressed because their husband
and father will not " say something religious " ere
he dies; whereupon the young clergyman comments
in his diary on the unreasonableness of demanding
that a man who all his life has been singularly reti-
cent of speech, but whose daily life was vocal with
his praise, should be expected in the throes of physi-
cal dissolution to grow suddenly eloquent on religious
topics, and edify the household.

The most noticeable thing about this journal is the
humble, self-depreciating way in which he invariably
speaks of his own performances.   This excessive self-
criticism is indeed somewhat painful to read, and
betrays that he was not in robust physical and men-
tal health when he thus wrote: " I can't lay aside
every weight, especially that weight of doubt whether
my hearers really care about what I am saying.  Per-
haps such doubts are wicked.  I ought to look deeper
and have more faith in man and truth and God."
Again he blames himself for his disposition to "inter-
nal scolding : " it must have been internal; certainly
no one ever heard it.  We find him walking out on
Saturday morning to gain energy and elasticity to
begin a second sermon for Sunday.  Perhaps he
does not find his topic or his text till noon, and then
works away tremendously till midnight upon it;
and the next day there were three services and the
Bible class to be conducted by the tired, frail young
preacher !  One Sunday it is bitterly cold, and only
twenty present at the morning service, and they have

no singing. In the afternoon the audience is even
less, and in the evening the church is quite empty, —
"only one pew full of giddy girls." He longs to
say something that shall touch these, but is "horri-
fied and utterly cast down" when a sudden explosive
laugh follows his "solemn closing adjuration." Lec-
turing on "Future Retribution," he says: "I en-
deavored to warn without frightening them; though
as for that," he adds, with quaint and character-
istic humor, "there is no danger of my ever fright-
ening anybody." He feels painfully the want of
co-operation and his own lack of organizing and
executive ability. He sighs, "Oh, what work in
such a climate to keep souls awake!" The dearth
of young men in the parish troubles him, and he
longs for "a young man like Kidder" in his society.
Nor were his anxieties and cares confined to his pas-
toral relation. For twenty years Mr. Brooks's sal-
ary was less than a thousand dollars annually. In
spite of his own self-denial and the economies of his
wife, this small sum became daily more inadequate
to their growing domestic needs. Four more chil-
dren were born to them, — Harriet Lyman, Jonathan
Mason, Mary Elizabeth, and Peyton Hazard Brooks.
Of these Jonathan Mason Brooks, a child of singu-
lar beauty, was a permanent invalid, and through
the eighteen years of his shadowed life required
and received the incessant care and lavish affec-
tion of his parents. They who were best acquainted
with the circumstances of Mr. Brooks's home-life
knew also that its daily trials and heroisms, so

patiently, loyally, sweetly borne, were among the
most beautiful testimonies to the excellence of his
character and the sincerity of his religious convic-
tions.    But even his rare powers of endurance must
have given way at times, had it not been for the sym-
pathy and strong sense of duty displayed by his
wife, the docility and promise of his remaining chil-
dren, and the thoughtful generosity of friends.

But while this overstrain of pastoral duties and
domestic cares seriously impaired his health and at
times dimmed the natural cheerfulness and hopeful-
ness of his disposition, there was another and brighter
side to his Newport life.  He keenly enjoyed his
home, and made it by example and teaching a cen-
tre of simple comfort, refined tastes, and genuine
good-will.  He entered with childlike relish into the
occupations and plays of his children, and when
they drew around the evening lamp, would read
aloud to them from the best books, construct pun-
ning or acrostic verses for their amusement, or join
gleefully in their youthful games.  One of the most
industrious and busy of men, he always seemed to
have ample leisure to bestow upon his children or
his friends.  He greatly delighted too in the charm-
ing scenery and romantic associations of his adopted
city.  As he walked with you about its quiet streets
he was full of interesting and quaint information
concerning its local reminiscences and ancient wor-
thies.  Hardly a beautiful feature in the landscape
of Aquidneck, — the "island of peace," as the Indians
called it, — or a notable event in its history, which his

graceful and melodious verse has not commemorated. If a depressed mood came over him he would take an exhilarating ramble over its pastures and beaches, stroll along the surf-beaten cliffs or through the rocky valleys of Paradise, or, climbing to Berkeley's Cave, he would sit, as did the good bishop before him, and watch the swell and tussle and foam of the waves as they broke in endless succession upon the shore below, and then return again to the unfinished sermon or parish duty with new heart and zest. The climate of Newport also, mild and genial, did much to prolong his life. It is hardly probable that if he had been settled elsewhere in New England, his slender frame could so long have endured its rigorous winters and blustering springs. If his congregation was somewhat exacting in earlier days in the amount of labor required of him, it looked up to him, as the years rolled on, with an ever-increasing confidence and affection. Always, too, Newport has been the chosen home of a little circle of cultivated and literary persons, in whose intercourse Mr. Brooks took particular pleasure, and who counted him among the chief attractions the place held for them. Among these were the hospitable and charming households of Samuel St. John and his noble wife, Mr. and Mrs. Henry Schroeder, Henry T. Tuckerman and his gifted son of the same name, Henry James the elder, — " a rare head and an excellent heart," as Mr. Brooks writes concerning him, — that veteran of American literature George W. Calvert, Col. T. W. Higginson, Edmund Tweedy, Samuel Powell, Francis Brinley,

George E. Waring, Jr., Benjamin H. Rhoades, Mrs.
McKaye, Miss Juliet H. Goodwin, and many others.

A class for the study of German literature, which
met under his direction, included many of the bright-
est young people of his parish and the general com-
munity, and was of great interest and value in their
higher culture.

Every summer witnessed the incoming of a large
number of wealthy, cultivated, and socially distin-
guished families from the principal American cities,
among whom Mr. Brooks formed most delightful
acquaintance and friendship, and from whom he re-
ceived abounding evidences of personal regard.   The
names of the Paines, Williams, Lows, Drakes, Crows,
Sturgises, Bancrofts, Nortons, Wales, Brewers, Bige-
lows, Appletons, Ticknors, Clarkes, Dr. S. G. and
Mrs. Howe, Charlotte Cushman and Margaret Foley,
and other friends of his earlier life in Newport,
are often mentioned in his papers and correspond-
ence with expressions of regard and affection.   He
maintained a lively correspondence with certain of the
friends already named, as well as with J. T. Fields, Dr.
Beck, the Rev. William R. Alger, George Bancroft,
Charles Eliot Norton, and with Count von Auersperg
(Anastasius Grün), Ferdinand Freiligrath, and other
German and American men of literature.   It is to be
regretted that this correspondence is either not of
sufficient general interest or is too defective to be
reproduced here.   His pulpit exchanges were but
few, and mostly with the Providence, Fall River,
and New Bedford ministers; but in the summer he

received occasional " spells," which he recalled with especial gratitude, from Dr. Burnap of Baltimore, Henry Giles, Augustus Woodbury, John Weiss, the Rev. Dr. F. H. Hedge, the Rev. Dr. Furness, and his two college mates and intimate life-long friends the Rev. Drs. Henry W. Bellows and Samuel Osgood of New York. The arrival of either of these clerical friends was always an occasion of joy to the gentle, loving minister at Newport; and we read in his journals of symposiums at which sermon-reading, mutual criticism, reminiscence, anecdote, and merry chat beguiled the quickly speeding hours. Once at least we have a glimpse of another welcome visitor : —

" Scribbled into doggerel a little of ' Faust,' in the midst of which I was called down ; and there stood Theodore Parker, large as life, with spectacles and pouting look, — the genius of an antique book. How glad I was to grasp the hand of my quondam fellow-student, hall-mate, brother-linguist, punster, German scholar, and general wag ! I forgot the present at once, and lived over again the old hall hours. He's just left town, — went off in the carryall with his basket of books. He gave me a most tantalizing glimpse of Tieck."

He was favored for only a few summers after his installation with the occasional presence and preaching of Dr. Channing in his pulpit. It was there the Doctor gave the sermon on the Sunday-school, printed in his works. Mr. Brooks tells us : —

" Of the four discourses he gave us in those last years I remember distinctly the subjects of three, — ' The Greatness of Human Nature,' ' Deliverance from Evil,' and ' Living to the Flesh.' I also recall very vividly his look and action in many instances; for example, in the first, the singular expressiveness of his gesture when he remarked how much more striking an impression it gave you of man's greatness to be able to fix the time of a comet's reappearance than (suiting the action to the word and stretching his slight arm to its full extent) it would if he could stretch forth his hand and touch a star.

"I have hoped in vain to see these and other great sermons of this luminous author, preached in the last years of his life, appear some day in print."

Another source of great enjoyment and recuperation were the vacation visits he annually made in later years, during the winter or spring, to the hospitable homes of certain of his summer parishioners and friends in other cities. Sometimes he found rest and tender care at the houses of his friends James Arnold of New Bedford and George W. Wales in Boston, or drank in the winter sunshine at the beautiful country-seat of his devoted and congenial acquaintance John E. Williams, at Irvington on the Hudson. In Philadelphia there was always a warm welcome for him at Robert Sturgis's and Dr. Furness's; in New York, at his friend Paine's. He sometimes went as far south as Baltimore to visit the Burnaps and Fricks. But there was no place to which he returned so often or so gladly, or in whose local associations he took so deep an interest as in his native city of Salem. His genial muse has embalmed in song many of the traditions and incidents of its civic and social life; and its homes, especially those of his sister Elizabeth and his brother Henry M. Brooks, always gave him a warm welcome.

In the fall of 1842 Mr. Brooks was afflicted with a severe bronchial trouble, and his friends anxiously urged him to seek a milder climate for the ensuing winter. The Unitarian faith had found a lodgment at that day in various cities of the South. At Mobile, Ala., the efforts of the ever-zealous St. Johns, of M. E. Martineau, a cousin of Harriet Martineau, and others had planted a promising Unitarian society. Mr. Brooks was invited to preach for them during the six months of winter and spring. The Newport parish consented to spare him, and the Rev. William Silsbee, his friend and classmate, ministered most acceptably in his stead. Mr. Brooks kept a minute journal of this Southern visit, from which we should be tempted to give some extracts, were it not for the limited space which the plan of this memoir allows us. It must be remarked, also, that partly from the characteristics of his own mind and partly from the delicacy of his position as a Northern clergyman visiting in a community proud, suspicious, and easily irritated at any comments upon the general aspects of their civilization or their peculiar institutions, his memoranda are chiefly of a personal nature, and contain little of wider interest. He notes with poetic feeling the picturesque local features of his new place of residence. The constant reference to climatic changes and the physical sensations they produced in him betray the invalid and health-seeker. He chronicles the incidents of his Sunday preaching, which, from the missionary character of the movement, was largely on doctrinal topics. He dwells upon the characters and ways of life of his new acquaintances, whose open-handed Southern hospitalities and demonstrative courtesy formed such a contrast to the reserved manners and repressed emotions of New Englanders. There was much leisure for reading and study. With the Toulmins and other of his new friends he brushed up his French, and in return made them acquainted with the German language and literature. He took long walks, and grows enthusiastic in his diary over the sunshine and blossom and fragrance of a Southern spring. Once he tries a buggy-ride, but with sorry results, and concludes, " I am sure I was not made for driving either horses or people." We find him reading a poem at a public dinner, amid the clatter of dishes, the popping of champagne corks, the blare of a brass band, and the echoes of fervid Southern oratory. The negroes are seldom alluded to, and for obvious reasons. He records, however, a grotesque theological discussion he was forced into with an unlettered African preacher. But we know that he returned home with an increased dislike to the institution of slavery. A delightful excursion was made to " lovely Pascagoula " during his stay. His journal bursts into poetry in its attempt to reproduce the wildness and sublimity of Nature, — the vast primeval forests, the morasses and bayous, the exquisite wild flowers, and the golden sunsets of that romantic region.

The "poor whites" interested him greatly, and he enlarges upon their angular appearance, uncouth dialect, rude manners, unwholesome fare, and camp-meeting fervor. But through all this succession of novel and enjoyable experiences runs the plaint of a homesick man, longing for the hour to arrive when his exile shall be ended and his own hearthstone and pulpit receive him back again to familiar and affectionate relations.

But the main resource and refreshment for Mr. Brooks, when overborne with parochial or private cares, were his literary studies and pursuits. Mr. Brooks was essentially a man of literature in his tastes and aspirations. Study was his favorite occupation, his solace and delight. When suffering from his oft-repeated infirmities, or oppressed with private or public cares, he would retire into the quiet of his library, and there lose himself in some new book, or woo the gentle muse of song, or plunge into the intricacies of a Jean Paul or Friedrich Rückert, and soon be entirely oblivious of all earthly trials and woes. Thus in one of his darkest hours, he tells us. he "was charmed and strengthened by reading again R. W. Emerson's famous Discourse."

Mr. Brooks wrote voluminously for the reviews and periodical press of his day, especially for the North American Review, the Christian Examiner, Harper's Monthly, Children's Friend, Diadem, Dayspring, Christian Register, Boston Transcript, and Newport and Salem newspapers. A list of the more important of these contributions, in their order of appearance, is given in the appendix to this memoir. He always entertained the ambition to write an English life of Martin Luther; and the thirty-six lectures on that great spiritual hero and his times which he read to his people at Newport were perhaps intended as material to this end. But it was as a poet, gifted by nature with a facile and graceful muse, that Mr. Brooks was best known to the world of American letters. Shining with a mild and genial ray, he became, from choice as well as disposition, the poet of the home life of his friends, contributing the wealth of his sympathetic imagination and the lyric sweetness of his verse to voice their joy or lift their sorrow. His versatility and productiveness were amazing. Literary and theological essays, reviews, historical monographs, odes and hymns for religious, patriotic, and festive occasions, drolleries, children's books, translations from the masterpieces of foreign literature, both in prose and rhyme, occasional verses and *jeux d'esprit*, flowed in a steady stream from his busy pen. This unlimited activity could not but affect unfavorably the quality of some of his literary work.

Mr. Brooks placed so modest a valuation upon his own powers as a poet that only the persuasion of his friends, and a desire to contribute to the interest of the annual fairs held by the ladies of his society, induced him to print, for their use on several occasions, a few of his original poems in book form.

It was as a translator from other languages that

Mr. Brooks was most widely known and esteemed in literary circles, both in this country and in Europe, and rendered most admirable service to the cause of English letters.

The qualities which distinguished Mr. Brooks as a German translator were his rare knowledge of the language and its literature, great practice in composition, a cultivated gift of expression, and a warm poetical sympathy. His first considerable publication was a translation of Schiller's drama " William Tell," which was printed in Providence in the year 1837. His collection of translated poems contributed to Ripley's " Specimens of Foreign Literature," and forming the fourteenth volume of the series, has already been alluded to. He was singularly happy in his rendering of shorter poems and lyrics; and it is not unlikely that his exquisite English versions of the ballads and songs of Uhland, Lenau, Chamisso, A. Grün, Freiligrath, and others, will longest preserve his literary reputation with posterity.

In 1842 there was published in Philadelphia his second collection of translated verse under the title " German Lyric Poetry." It contained also contributions from H. W. Longfellow, John S. Dwight. Samuel Osgood, and others. In 1845 was printed the poem which Mr. Brooks read before the Phí Beta Kappa. A little volume consisting of an English version of Schiller's " Homage to the Arts" and other poems, original and translated, was printed for the benefit of the Church Fair of 1846. A similar volume appeared in 1848, entitled " Aquidneck,"

after the principal poem in the book, in which may
be found some of the best poetic writing of Mr.
Brooks, many of the lines being of great power and
beauty.

"The Old Stone Mill Controversy" is a valuable
historical monograph, summing up the local testi-
mony concerning that curious relic of the past. In
the same year in which this little work appeared
(1851), the condition of Mr. Brooks's throat com-
pelled him to seek another respite at the South ;
and for a second time we find him ministering to
the still shepherdless flock at Mobile. Returning
late in the spring of the following year, he resumed
his pastoral and literary labors. Another collection
of original verse, "Songs of Field and Flood,"
was printed for the Ladies' Fair of 1853. He also
revised at this time his first volume of translated
poems ; and it appeared at Boston under the new
title, "German Lyrics." In the mean time he was
hard at work, in the intervals of parish duty, on
his version of Goethe's "Faust," begun long before,
and also of Richter's "Titan." Innumerable were
the calls upon him by editors, composers, parish
committees, literary societies, and private collectors
for contributions in verse and prose. To all such
demands Mr. Brooks yielded but too readily. It
seemed impossible for him to return a negative to
any appeal for his services. His health, always deli-
cate, subjected to the double strain of overwork and
the rigorous New England climate, now threatened
to give way entirely. A malady of the chest and

throat totally disabled him for pulpit service. It
became evident that he needed an entire change of
climate and long exemption from pastoral and lit-
erary work. Through the generous intervention of
a friend, a shipowner, it was determined that he
should take the long sea-voyage to India and re-
turn. He felt it a sore trial to exile himself again,
and for so long a period, from home and congenial
duties ; yet the scenic and historical features of the
Far East appealed to his imagination, and greatly
attracted him. Accordingly he set sail, on the 27th
of October, 1853, for Madras and Calcutta in the
new ship " Piscataqua" of Portsmouth, N. H., of five
hundred and forty-nine tons' register, her lower hold
containing a cargo of ice, with three hundred tons
of miscellaneous freight stowed in her 'tween-decks.
Three returning missionaries with their families com-
prised his fellow-passengers. As was his custom
when travelling, Mr Brooks kept an extended diary,
which is interesting but painful reading ; for the
voyage proved anything but restorative to the health
of our friend. Shortly after her departure from Bos-
ton harbor, the vessel was caught by a gust of wind
on the port tack, and heeled over ; the ice in her
hold, improperly stowed, listed ; and for the remain-
der of the voyage of one hundred and forty-three days
she was on her beam-ends, looking like a ship about
to capsize. Unable to walk upright, or with any
degree of comfort on her decks, except when she
was on a tack with a fresh breeze blowing, wearied
with the long duration of the journey, and fearing

4

in every gale that they would go to the bottom, her unfortunate passengers suffered intensely. Mr. Brooks's invalidism made him less able to cope with the discomforts and trials of the journey. He was afflicted with a distressing cough; he could not lie at ease in his berth, but was violently thrown about or hunched up in an angle of it. He was compelled to listen for long weeks to the chafing and quarrelling of the weary sailors, and, worse than all, to attend the daily religious services of his fellow-passengers, whose gloomy Calvinistic sermons, morbid prayers, and lurid, ghastly hymns intensified the cheerlessness and terror of the situation. This part of his journal is largely a chronicle of his physical miseries, his homesickness, and longing for release. Fortunately, thoughtful friends had provided him with a chest of books, largely works of travel and information concerning the countries he was to pass *en route* or to visit. In the diligent study of these books, and the daily instruction he received from his fellow-passengers in Tamil and Hindostanee in exchange for the lessons in Hebrew and German and Italian which he gave them, he found a partial relief from the insufferable tedium of the journey, and also added to his considerable stock of languages. As they sailed into tropical zones the aspects of sea and sky became more varied and interesting, and his ailments decreased. He notes the curious specimens of animal life which now hovered in the wake of the ship, and tries his hand with the rest at a novel kind of fishing for dolphin,

booby, and albatross. Always an expert though
untrained draughtsman, as they near the coasts of
India and Ceylon he traces in his journal the out-
lines of headland and mountain, the surf-beaten
shores, and dimly discerned villages and fortresses
along their route. It need hardly be said that his
various moods of elation or depression at the experi-
ences of this voyage found their congenial expression
in frequent versification.

On the 17th of March the luckless craft at length
arrived in the harbor of Madras, to the great joy of the
passengers and crew, and the wonderment of all who
beheld her sorry condition. Mr. Brooks was received
with warm welcome and unbounded hospitalities by
former Salem friends and by the resident English, to
whom he brought letters of introduction. It would
be pleasant to insert here some passages from his
journal, which is full of the novel sights and sensa-
tions to which he was now introduced. But again we
must deny ourselves, in view of the plan of this brief
memoir. Mr. Brooks visited India for health rather
than information; and this, with his poetic tempera-
ment, which took little interest in practical affairs,
makes of his daily journal a record of personal im-
pressions instead of a series of studies of Indian life
and institutions likely to be of permanent value.[1]
Yet, as we should suppose from a writer of his tal-
ent, the pictures he draws of the scenery and life about

[1] These impressions are well summed up in an article he
contributed to Harper's Monthly Magazine for December, 1857,
— "Madras in Pictures."

him are full of color and animation. He describes
the splendid temples and palaces and the lordly state
of the ruling classes; the squalid, crowded quarters
of the natives; the varied and picturesque move-
ment of the great city, as the living tides of its
diverse populations pour through the bazaars and
squares and lanes; the gentry rolling in their costly
equipages along the esplanade; the beggars abjectly
crouching by the wayside; the half-naked boatmen
fiercely contending on the beach; the heathen wor-
shipper prostrate before his idols. He marks the vast
expanse of the bay, heaving and tossing in the glar-
ing sunlight, and the rollers breaking with thun-
derous roar upon the yellow sands. We see him
attending the ceremonious, elaborate dinners of the
resident English, with their crowd of dusky ser-
vants, highly seasoned dishes, fiery wines, and sway-
ing punkas gently beating the air into waves of
coolness. At evening he sits in the door of his
bungalow, and sketches the features of the country
home whose hospitalities he is enjoying. He listens
to the chatter, watches the sinuous movements, and
studies the costumes and countenances of the Orien-
tals who swarm about the enclosure. The wild luxu-
riance and exuberance of tropical vegetation amaze
and overwhelm him. The brilliant and busy days,
with their sweltering heat and press of life, are suc-
ceeded by still, cool nights; but he is early awakened
by the tremendous uproar with which in tropical
countries the animal creation from field and wood
greets the sun's rising. His interest in the religious

aspects of Indian life is naturally great. With his hosts he attends divine worship in the Established and the Presbyterian churches, but is not much edified. He visits the mission-houses and schools, and has long talks with missionaries and Hindu converts, and especially interesting interviews with certain Mussulman nawabs, or nobles, whom he also visits in their homes.

There was in Madras at this time a Unitarian theistic mission, established and conducted by a Mr. Roberts, a native minister, whose work Mr. Brooks was specially commissioned by the American Unitarian Association to examine and report upon. This he did very faithfully, visiting his chapel and school, addressing the members of the little flock, and encouraging both minister and people to remain loyal to the simple faith of Jesus, and resist the great pressure that was brought to bear upon them from both heathen and Christian sources. On his return Mr. Brooks successfully interceded in their behalf with his fellow-Unitarians in New England, writing among other things an article in the Christian Examiner, " India's Appeal to Christian Unitarians."

An interesting episode of his stay at Madras was his visit to the Seven Temples by the Sea, whither he was borne in a palanquin by the natives, and gazed with wondering awe upon those mighty, crumbling memorials of a vast antiquity.

Four weeks had passed rapidly away, crowded with interest and incident; and the " Piscataqua," now on an even keel, sailed with our friend once more, a passenger for Calcutta. Here another three weeks were passed, but they did not prove as enjoyable to him as his previous experience. The season was more advanced, and the fierce heat of summer, from which he had suffered much at Madras, now became intolerable. He was wearied with sight-seeing, his throat gave returning symptoms of distress; and his homesickness, though abated, was not relieved by the letters from his wife and children, from his beloved sister-in-law Miss Emily L. Hazard, from Arnold, Calvert, Norton, Tuckerman, and other dear friends, which he found awaiting him at Calcutta. He was not sorry, therefore, when his Oriental holiday came to an end, and he set sail on the "Lotus," — a fine vessel, with better accommodations, — and after a prosperous voyage landed in Boston on Sunday, Aug. 27, 1854, just ten months after he first set out for India's coral strand.

Making his way to the First Church, on Chauncey Street, he sat with grateful heart in a pew of the old meeting-house, and lifted his thanksgiving to Almighty God, who had so tenderly preserved him from the dangers of the sea and land, and brought him back again to his own country and kindred.

It became apparent, however, that while his recent experiences had been very stimulating to his mental powers, he had received but little physical recuperation from them. His throat was still in a very delicate condition, and unable to bear the strain of preaching. He made the attempt on Sunday, Sept.

17, 1854, but for a year thereafter was compelled to
suspend his pulpit duties. The Rev. F. A. Tenney
acted as his substitute, and the relation between them
was of a most intimate and friendly character. Mean-
while Mr. Brooks was not idle. His pastoral relation
was nearer his heart than ever, and his pen was never
without congenial employment. He gave himself to
his German studies with especial zeal at this time,
completing his versions of "Faust" and "Titan,"
and beginning a rendering of Rückert's "Wisdom of
the Brahmin," besides translating many lesser poems
from that language. After an absence from his pul-
pit of nearly two years in all, he returned to it again,
and talked to his flock about the mutual relation of
minister and people. He tells them he has had
abundant occasion during this time to reflect on this
theme, and wisely thinks that "congregations can
more easily be extravagant in the quantity of preach-
ing they require, than ministers are likely to be in
their solicitude about the quality of what they offer."

In 1856 appeared the first considerable fruit of Mr.
Brooks's scholarship, his translation of the First Part
of Goethe's "Faust." In this work his gifts as a trans-
lator were most strikingly displayed. To render this
masterpiece of German literature into a befitting Eng-
lish dress in the original metres and in rhyme was a
yet untried and prodigiously difficult undertaking.
All succeeding translations owe a deep but too often
unacknowledged obligation to Mr. Brooks's version
of "Faust," concerning which the poet Longfellow, in
a congratulatory letter under date of Nov. 4, 1856,

writes, that it "gives the reader a better and more complete idea of it than any other translation." Similar praise has been accorded it by many competent critics, notably by George Ripley in the "New York Tribune," and by a writer in the "New Englander," some years since, in a formal article on the subject. Although this translation passed through several editions, it was not a successful publication in the financial returns it brought him. But it was certainly a noteworthy contribution to American literature, and won him the appreciation of the select few for whose esteem he most cared.

In 1859 Mr. Brooks published a volume of sermons under the title "The Simplicity of Christ's Teachings." To estimate his powers as a preacher from this volume and the writer's own reminiscences of him, his discourse in the pulpit was characterized by simplicity and clearness, a gentle earnestness that persuaded rather than convicted his hearers, and a serene and tender piety which at times rose to fervent assurance or deepened into holy awe. His style of sermonizing was practical and hortatory, felicitous in diction, imaginative, with many illustrations drawn from Nature, and a large insistence on the sayings and tropes of the Bible, and all suffused with the graciousness and devoutness of his own amiable and saintly character. His voice was not strong, and a little dry in its tones; and his delivery, with little or no gesture, was not sufficiently animated to be deeply impressive. Yet there was something indescribably winning in his pulpit presence. What he said in his

college journal of Dr. Gannett's preaching, "I liked
the man better than his manner," might have been
applied to his own sermonizing. The gospel which he
preached he looked and was, and this of itself drew
the hearts of his hearers unto him. His appearance
in the principal pulpits of the denomination was
always a welcome one, and he did not lack for pro_
posals to remove to other fields of labor where larger
following and emolument awaited him. The general
appreciation of his merits as a sermonizer was shown
by his selection to preach the annual sermon before
the graduating class at the Harvard Divinity School
in the year 1860. His theme was "The Christian
Minister the Man of God." Its drift lies in the brief
sentences we extract from it : " He who would make
full proof of his ministry must make full proof of his
manhood;" and again, "The vocation of the minister
is to express and educate the man." The sermon
closes with a beautiful tribute to his friend Theodore
Parker, then just dead at Florence.

In the mean time the war clouds, which for some
years past had been ominously gathering on the
horizon of American political life, suddenly swept
across the skies in dense masses, and burst in fury
upon the devoted land. Mr. Brooks felt that another
trial of his manhood and ministry was impending,
perhaps the greatest of all. Newport was intensely
loyal to the Union, and her sons were not backward
in enlisting in its behalf. A hospital barrack and
convalescent camp for five thousand soldiers was
established at Portsmouth Grove, on the island. The

fort was heavily garrisoned, war ships lay in the commodious harbor, and the United States Naval Academy was removed from Annapolis to Newport during the continuance of the war. The Unitarian pulpit during these trying and critical times never failed to echo and sometimes to lead the patriotic spirit of the community. The titles of the sermons Mr. Brooks preached during those years are an earnest of this : " Be collected, sober, and hopeful in these times ; " " The Temper we need ; " " Be strong, fear not ; " " The Mountain to which the Nation has come ; " " Our duty in these times, — a patient mind, a cheerful heart, a hopeful spirit." In 1863 we find him writing to a friend : " I still have to preach war, and sometimes I am ready to give out. I am naturally such a peace man."

But while united on the general question of the preservation of the Union, there was some diversity of opinion in his parish on the subject of emancipating the slaves. Never an extremist in opinion or violent in uttering his convictions, Mr. Brooks was yet a firm antislavery man, and in previous years the incidental statement of his views in the pulpit had awakened much displeasure in the congregation. He now felt it incumbent upon him to speak more freely and boldly on this subject. In his Fast Day sermon for 1861 he affirms that Government must declare emancipation a military necessity, or if the alienated States rejoin the Union it must be as free States. " No laws or institutions should oppress any class of God's children. The oppressor should cease

from his oppression, and the enslaved go free. Such
is the fast that God hath chosen " Much feeling
was produced by this and other "Abolition" dis-
courses. Certain influential parishioners threatened
to withdraw entirely from his ministrations. At the
close of a sermon in which he had gently but faith-
fully borne his testimony to human rights, a leading
member of his society said to him, "I have felt for
some time that you must go, but now I am sure of
it!" "Sir," quietly replied the firm though gentle
preacher, "I hold my hat in my hand." But he did
not go. Events preached emancipation more strongly
than he. A few persons left the congregation, but
more stayed and were converted to a larger concep-
tion of human brotherhood. On Thanksgiving Day,
1864, when the light was beginning to break over
the distracted land, his topic divides itself into the
three heads, "grateful for the past, diligent in the
present, vigilant for the future."

" Our text is written on the soil of a land reconsecrated
by the blood of a new army of martyrs; it is written on
the sky into which the smoke of a nation's sacrifice for
freedom and righteousness and humanity is still ascending ;
it is written on millions of hearts that have passed through
agitating and sad experiences of Divine chastening and
mercies, — and whoso will pause and listen to the still
small voice of the inner witness shall hear the Holy Spirit
interpreting, expounding, and applying the text I speak of
to every freeman's conscience."

Again he rejoices over the re-election of Mr. Lin-
coln. "A good Providence guided the choice of the

people," he declares, and praises "the healthful simplicity of his unsophisticated good-nature. A man in understanding; in malice a child."

His literary labors were interrupted but not entirely suspended by the absorbing events and duties of the Civil War. In 1862, in the midst of its strife and agony, appeared his translation of Jean Paul Richter's "Titan," which had long been seeking a publisher. Richter is one of the most obscure and involved of German writers. If we may accept the dictum that a translator should be akin, if not equal, in spirit to him whom he seeks to reproduce, then the great German was certainly fortunate in his interpreter. Mr. Brooks himself possessed many of the qualities of the author he so much admired, — the lively fancy, romantic imagination, tender sentiment, the grotesque humor and moral enthusiasm, which are displayed in the Titan, Hesperus, Invisible Lodge, Selina, History of Fibel, and other works of Jean Paul which Mr. Brooks translated, and some of which remain still in manuscript. His rendering of "Titan" was in every respect an admirable one, and drew forth the following appreciative, commendatory letter from Carlyle, himself a translator of Richter's works : —

CHELSEA, 16 March, 1863.

DEAR SIR, — Several months ago you made me a very pretty and a very welcome gift, your excellent *Translation of Titan*, which surely I ought to have acknowledged sooner ; but the truth is, I am frightfully driven about in these months and years, and have seldom time to write a Note even to friends.

Finding your Translation of such quality, I took steadily to reading it, — steadily gave myself about an hour of it, the last thing every night, by way of washing down the bitter dusts of the day with a cup of right wine before going to bed! I am sorry it is done long since, for indeed I had not had any such reading for years back, and could not but acknowledge, spite of all my criticisms, that here was more of real human stuff than in all the novels written in my time. The Book is beautifully printed, too, every way an exquisite handful for a good reader.

You have been wonderfully successful : have caught a good deal of the *tune* of Jean Paul, and have unwinded his meaning, in general, with perfect accuracy, into comfortable clearness, out of those coils he involves it in. I did not keep the original *open* all the way, but had a feeling that I was safe in your hands. One or two little specks I did notice, — nothing of any consequence : — Boouvert, whom you call " The German Gentleman," is in reality the *Teutsche* ORDENS *Herr*, that is to say, a " Teutonic Knight," — imaginary in everything.[1]

I once read " fixings " too in some speech; do make it "trimmings " or any equivalent English word ; " fixings " came like a momentary splash of cold water on the skin ; painfully reminding one, " Ha, it is *not* Jean Paul's self that you are reading then, it is an American *Translation* of Jean Paul ! "

In conclusion I will congratulate you on having added a highly recognizable new item of good reading for the whole

[1] The translator was aware of this, and used the word "Gentleman" in the most general sense, as we call a Senator "The Honorable Gentleman." Besides, to call him the *Knight* might have confounded him with Gaspard, who was also called thus.

English genealogy of us (now a most extensive Body of People in this world) ; — and with the hope of perhaps seeing a *Hesperus* from you some day, and certainly with many thanks, I remain

Yours sincerely,

T. CARLYLE.

On the 29th of March, 1863, the hearts of the parents were saddened and yet relieved by the death of their unfortunate child, for so many years, by day and by night, the object of their incessant and tender care. Joy followed sorrow in the humble minister's household when, in October of the same year, their eldest daughter, Harriet, went forth from it a happy bride, with the blessing of her parents. Long before translated, but now first published, was Kortum's satirical poem, "The Jobsiad." The "Knittelverse" of the original, with its rollicking humor and quaint turns of expression, are admirably reproduced in Mr. Brooks's doggerel verse. In 1864 a second work of Richter's, "Hesperus," was translated and published in two volumes. As a literary task it had great merit; as a financial venture it yielded slight returns. Indeed, this was true of nearly all Mr. Brooks's literary undertakings. With small knowledge of the popular demand, he chose for translation usually such works as he found himself in spiritual affinity with, or which satisfied his literary judgment. The result was that he gained more credit for scholarship than pecuniary reward from his labors with the pen.

It now became apparent, however, that all this work, added to the mental strain of war-time, was seriously impairing his health and threatening him with loss of voice if not of eyesight. His physician ordered an entire cessation from pulpit duty for a year, and, if possible, a change of climate. It had always been the darling wish of his heart to visit Europe, and now the way was providentially opened. On the 11th of October, 1865, having received another leave of absence from his indulgent parish, and with his heart lightened by the assurance that it would be well with his family and church during his enforced absence, Mr. Brooks sailed for England. On the same steamer with him were his friends the Rev. Samuel Longfellow and Ernest Longfellow, together with other acquaintances. Among the letters of sympathy and farewell which he received was one from the Rev. John Weiss, then deep in his Shakspearean studies, expressing the wish that this time his *berth* might indeed prove " a sleep and a forgetting." Mr. Brooks kept, as usual, a copious diary of this trip; but, mindful of the prescribed limits of this memoir, the commonness now-a-days of American travel abroad, and the personal nature of most of his entries, we but sparsely avail ourselves of its interesting observations and experiences. Arriving at Liverpool on a Sunday, he sought the service of the Rev. John Hamilton Thom, — "a man of mild, somewhat melancholy countenance, and eyes of sweet though sad and thoughtful tenderness," — with whose preaching he was greatly delighted. The

Rev. Philip Wicksteed, another Unitarian clergyman
of Liverpool, — " with a merry face, twinkling eyes,
and mellow, musical voice," — gave him a warm re-
ception.   He also visited the Gaskells — "lovely
people " — and Prof. Goldwin Smith.   It was his
first European visit, and he was eager as a boy
to behold the sights and meet, if possible, some of
the eminent men of England.   At Chester he saw
his first cathedral, and was profoundly impressed by
it, and deeply interested also in the Roman antiqui-
ties of the town.   At Oxford his scholarly tastes
were gratified by a visit to the Bodleian Library
and colleges.   It was the day of Lord Palmerston's
funeral.   The bells tolled, and a solemn procession
moved through the streets.   Arriving in London,
his first care was to seek out Chelsea and call on
Thomas Carlyle.   Their interview was so character-
istic and is so well told that we cannot deny our
readers the pleasure of it : —

" Found him at breakfast.   While the two old servant-
women were whispering where they should put me, a voice
as familiar as if I had heard it from childhood bade me
walk through, and there sate the great man munching his
toast before the fire, — a little, wizened-faced, Irish-looking
man, with a cheek like a frozen apple, and eyes bright as
the cauld blue north.   With what a queer smile he greeted
me !   Soon in talking he came, apropos of Jean Paul, upon
the subject of his first introduction to the world of German
literature.   Got his first inklings from Madame de Staël.
At that time he was perplexed about the problems of man
and the universe, and, fancying the Germans could help him,

undertook to learn the language of an old German Jew, —
could not get any help from him, never heard of any-
body's learning anything from him, did n't believe the
man knew German himself. At last a mariner brought
home among some packages sheets of Schiller's works, and
with these he worked his way into the language and litera-
ture. Then he showed me two autographs of Jean Paul.
Had I seen Emerson ? Yes, two days before I sailed. At
this 'the creatur' gave an eldritch grin ' — 'to think of see-
ing Emerson in the flesh,' and afterwards, upstairs, he re-
peated it to his wife with that chuckle reminding me so of
Henry Giles's : ' Wife, here is a man who has seen Emerson
in the flesh !' 'A nice man, Emerson,' he then said, very
quietly and respectfully, but could n't make out the secret of
his notions about our country. Then he launched out into
his disagreeable strain of screaming away about the *Nagur*,
— a fat, lazy brute, sprawling about here on God's earth
for no sort of good, etc. ; laughed at a set of exiles here in
London, who think if they can only get everybody a vote,
the world is cured. He certainly talked like one who had
no moral sentiment. Speaking later with Goldwin Smith
about that high-horse style of talking in which Carlyle in-
dulges, I asked, ' Does n't he sometimes see through the joke
of it all himself?' 'No,' said he; 'it is a serious business
with him.' I could n't help laughing, but not so grimly
as he did all the while, and could only say, 'Ah, you should
be one of us to appreciate our position and necessities in this
crisis. It is the real Puritan element fighting for its exist-
ence.' With that he went into his usual eulogy of the
Puritan, and finally lighted his long pipe, sticking the bowl
away into the chimney. Soon he took me up to see his
wife, saying, 'Here is the translator of " Titan." ' She wore
a sad smile, and seemed a woman of small health and few
words. But Conway says she talks fast enough when Car-

lyle is away.  He showed me his pictures, — a big one of little Prince Fred, drumming and walking with his sister; one of Cromwell; Luther's mother and father, Scotch-looking old people; and so on.  Bidding good-by to the strange man, I went my way."

Moncure D. Conway, whose well-known kindness to Americans visiting London was quickened in this case by a sincere personal friendship with Mr. Brooks, was his companion and guide about the city, and did much to make his brief stay profitable and pleasant. He introduced him to Peter Taylor, Esq., the eminent Liberal member of Parliament from Chelsea, at whose fine old mansion he gained pleasant insight into the charming hospitality, broad culture, and solid worth of the higher English middle class.

Dr. James Martineau's preaching was all that he had anticipated and more.  In the afternoon he went to hear Dean Stanley at Westminster Abbey on Lord Palmerston, but was able to catch but little of the discourse, owing to the crowd and his distance from the speaker.  The liturgy, however, and especially the responses rising and falling in the gray-grown walls of the Abbey, like the waves of the sea in some vast cavern, deeply impressed him.  With Conway and Samuel Longfellow he made a second visit to the philosopher of Cheyne Walk : —

" We met Neuberg, who translates Carlyle into German. It was droll to hear him combine the German accent with Carlyle's rising slide, which he has caught.  They raised a great pother over their tea-making.  Carlyle said that Jean Paul had grown less of a hero to him, but his human sympathy he did love. He talked of Palmerston and suffrage, and showed us a wonderful daguerreotype of a head of Cromwell. He thought it the finest human face he had ever seen, and that there was something most touching in its union of conscious strength with heavenly sweetness. We broke up at ten, Conway staying to have some private talk."

Another pleasure in store for him was the meeting with the German poet Freiligrath, then residing in London, whom he greatly admired, and many of whose lyrics he had rendered into English. Freiligrath received him with true German heartiness, invited him to his charming home, showed him many interesting memorials and relics of the poets Goethe, Schiller, Rückert, and others, and equipped him with valuable letters of introduction to friends on the Continent. The presence of the cholera at Paris made him undecided as to his future course of travel, when Mr. and Mrs. Paine, dear friends and summer parishioners, invited him to accompany them on a journey to the Netherlands and Germany. The little party set out for Dover and Brussels, visiting Canterbury Cathedral *en route*. His journal contains charming sketches of what is now much travelled ground, — Belgium and Holland and their towns and villages, farms and peasant life, dykes and windmills, their monuments and churches and pictures. Hanover and Bremen were visited, and a week passed in Berlin, not then as imposing a city as the events of the last twenty years have made it. At Wittenberg he came upon historically familiar ground, the haunts of his spiritual hero Martin Luther. At Leipzig it was the great memory of John Sebastian Bach which was most present with him. He attends afternoon church, and is surprised to find hardly thirty worshippers in the huge edifice. " Lutheranism seems, like an old tree, to have dropped its fruits far away from it, and itself to stand desolate," is his comment. At Weimar he visits with profound emotion the places made forever memorable in literary history as the scenes of the life and labors of Herder, Goethe, Schiller, Wieland, and other illustrious writers and men.

It may be imagined with what deep, enthusiastic interest Mr. Brooks visited the shrines and beheld the memorials of these lofty minds, with whose thoughts and ideals his own spirit had been for so many years in intimate communion, and whose masterpieces he had through his translations made accessible to a larger circle of readers. The companions of his journey relate that his delight in all he saw and learned was as genuine and ardent as a child's. Certainly all who knew Mr. Brooks's interest in German literature, or who have felt themselves under obligations to him for his labors as a translator, will rejoice that towards the close of his industrious and unselfish life he was granted this most congenial reward of his scholarly toil. Dresden and Prague were the next places of pilgrimage, and exercised their contrasted fascinations upon him. We find him enraptured with the quaintness of old Nuremburg, and at Frankfort on the Main happy in the genial company of German friends, to whom his faithful Newport parishioners

the Finkenstädts had given him letters of introduc-
tion. The "Gemüthlichkeit" of German home-life,
its heartiness, simplicity, absence of reserve, and cheer-
ful companionship, greatly attracted and charmed him.
Other lands might excel Germany in scenic and ven-
erable historic interest, but nowhere was there for
him so unaffected and cordial a greeting, and in no
foreign people was his heart so warmly enlisted as
in the fellow-countrymen of his literary favorites,
Richter, Rückert, and Goethe.

A vision of Heidelberg Castle and the valley of
the Neckar, a day at Strasburg, and he faced north-
ward to Paris, where he spent a busy, enjoyable month,
of which, however, no other record appears among his
papers than that on the 7th of December, 1865, he
celebrated with the American Colony a Thanksgiving
dinner at the Grand Hotel, and read a poem which
he had prepared for the occasion.

Mr. Brooks's impatience to continue his journey
southward overcame all fears of the lingering cholera,
and he proceeded by way of Marseilles and the Med-
iterranean to Rome, in which city we find him in
February, 1866, and where with the exception of a de-
lightful excursion in May to Naples, Capri, Pompeii,
and other places in that neighborhood, he remained
for several months.

As this was his most prolonged stay, so it is also
the one concerning which his note-books give the
most detailed and interesting account. The resident
Americans, to whom he was known either in person
or as a man of literature, received him with great

cordiality, while he found among the travellers tem-
porarily sojourning in Rome a number of parish-
ioners and friends.   The hospitable home of the
Goulds was ever open to him, and from the artist
and poet W. W. Story, his native townsman, he
received many courtesies.   Charlotte Cushman, the
eminent actress and later his esteemed parishioner
at Newport, the Gardner Brewers, Terrys, McChes-
neys, and other old-time acquaintance gave him a
warm greeting; and their friendly chat relieved some-
what the homesickness which he confesses tormented
him even among the crowded experiences and novel
and fascinating impressions of his Roman days.   He
spent much time in the studios, where the gentle,
genial poet, with his ruddy countenance and seraphic
look, was a great favorite with the artists.   Over-
beck and Rossetti were charmed with his genuine
admiration of art.   Harriet Hosmer, Rogers, Free-
man, the many-sided artist Ball, Tilton, Edmonia
Lewis, Sarah Clarke, and especially Margaret Foley,
became his friends and intimates during his stay.
The 22d of February, Washington's Birthday, was
celebrated by the Americans in Rome with a Public
Breakfast, at which one hundred and seventy-two per-
sons were present.   Minister King presided; Story
and Freeman discoursed about art and America; the
Rev. Phillips Brooks spoke with impetuous eloquence
on the Union; and our Newport preacher read a
poem, which was well received.   He had secured a
lodging high up in the fourth story of an ancient
house, so as to be nearer the sky and sun, and re-

moved as much as possible from the noisy street-clatter of an Italian city. It did not hide him entirely from bores and beggars, however. These soon discovered his amiable helplessness in their presence, and how easily his heart was touched by any display of human misery. He gives a half-humorous account of a Signora D——, who persistently climbed to his abode for a number of days in succession to secure his influence in behalf of a subscription concert to be given by herself. In loud, strident tones, and with much dramatic gesticulation, she poured forth, day after day, her recital of domestic miseries and needs; on each occasion departing with a fresh batch of letters of introduction to various members of the American colony with whom Mr. Brooks had become acquainted. He is subjected to considerable good-humored badinage concerning the concert to be given " under his patronage." When the fatal evening arrives Mr. Brooks resignedly dons his best suit and drives to the concert-room, but, failing to look closely at his ticket, gives a wrong direction to the coachman, and is taken to a distant part of the city. Discovering his mistake, he is driven hurriedly back to the right palazzo, only to find that the concert is over and the lights are out, and to be laughed at next morning by his friends because of his evident unwillingness to " face the music."

His meals were either brought to his rooms or taken at an Italian restaurant near by, which he frequented in order better to study the people and learn their language. Here is a graphic picture of the latter resort : —

"Our dinner to-day in della Croce was a singular affair. There were, beside my Irish friend and my American self and our two Austrian padronas and the Italian husband, the brother of the latter and his wife, with the children at the cats-table, and two old Italian gentlemen of the old school, one of them very talkative and quizzical ; and finally dropped in, to the great glee of all, a young friar, Padre Paolo, as they called him. Such a cluck and clatter ! the servant-maids and big nurse now and then putting in their word and gesture and joining in the fun; and the dog Volantino withal, justifying Burns's word,

> ' And I for joy ha' barkit wi' 'em,'

kept up a howl and dog laugh all round under the table. It was, I suppose, a fine specimen of jolly Italian domestic life. Some of the dishes were as queer as the gabble. The frittos (Anglice *fritters*) were a suggestion of croquettes and cod in one. It was refreshing after an hour of the half-intelligible chatter to go and cool my eyes and quiet my senses in the shade of one of the great rooms of the many-roomed house."

On another occasion he "took tea in a desperate mood at the Roma, and in consequence had one of my old-fashioned bad dreams of getting to church without any sermon, and having to dodge about and dive into a chest under the porch for a handful of manuscript ones. So much for green tea ! "

Mr. Brooks's Roman days were passed in the usual round of sight-seeing, visiting the famous ruins, monuments, churches, museums, and art collections

of the Eternal City, with pleasant excursions into the
surrounding country. One of the latter, an excur-
sion to Tivoli, in company with Margaret Foley, Mrs.
Freeman, and a party of friends, is so charmingly
told that in spite of its length it shall be inserted
here : —

"We drove out through the Porta San Lorenzo and by
the old church of the same name. At the city gate was a
goodly swarm of country people, contadinas and boys and
babies collected, one crowd engaged in an excited but ap-
parently not angry altercation with an official in regard to
taxable articles which they might be supposed to have
among them. One little woman seemed to be the spokes-
man of the party and tribune of the people, and she walked
round the men with so much eager eloquence of tongue and
fingers that red-stripe was evidently coming off second best
and about beating a good-natured retreat. Sun and dust,
particularly the latter, which was aggravated by the high
walls and hedges that shut in the Roman roads, were a
great drawback to our enjoyment and intelligent apprecia-
tion of the natural beauty and monumental and historic
impressiveness of the eighteen miles of Campagna which
stretched between us and the mountains. Still we did
enjoy a vast deal, — the flowers, particularly the bright red
poppies that lined the roadside and nodded on the walls
and rocks or colored the hills ; the strings of cattle on the
last lines of the upland meadow, standing out against the
background of the far mountains, in the hollows of which
Frascati and other villages showed white and picturesque ;
Monte Cavo, rising in its historic impressiveness ; then, by
and by, Tivoli itself, stretching with its cluster of gray
roofs away up the ravine among these high and solemn
mountains, on the peaks of which the clouds were clinging

and crawling. Far away to the left we beheld the two
green peaks and the two castle towns of San Angelo and
Monticello, with huddles of gray houses and battlements
crowning the crags up to the foot of which climbs the
luxurious green, — the beautiful Anio crossing and recross-
ing our path with its olive-green waters ; these, and so
many other objects of interest, were not wholly lost upon
us. As we approached Tivoli, the round silver shield of
the moon stood over the rocky cone that towered above the
town on the right. The sun was sinking far across the
Campagna with a golden glow. We passed by the road-
side several ancient tombs, one a mere shell ; another with
a chimney attached to it and made into a hut of habita-
tion ; the third somewhat resembling that of Cecilia Me-
tella, only in a more complete state of preservation and
restoration, — that of the Plautus family, with long inscrip-
tions on tomb and tablet. At last, just as the sun sank,
we entered on the road that winds up hill through the ex-
tensive woods of strange-looking old olive-trees, their black
stems, so thinned and twisted with age and decrepitude,
contorted into the most grotesque and mimic shapes and
attitudes and actions, some representing dancers, waltzers,
others wrestlers, broadsword-fighters. There were affrighted
beings in the act of flying from Troy or Pompeii; there
was Æneas, and Anchises, and Creusa. There were poor,
old, lame, halt, crippled veterans ; old fellows standing
with their legs astraddle in the most painful positions, —
some apparently on their last legs, and yet it seemed as
if there never could have been any that died among them.
And through this ghostly and ghastly multitude far away
the red sky gleamed and Peter's dome looked in from the
wide distance — what an evening ! Now and then the
people had walled up a bank where the crumbling of
some old temple or tomb threatened to carry away their

dear old olive-trees. Here and there in the midst of the
sombre wood, bits of ancient mosaic pavement cropped out
like geological strata. Through this still, sombre, solemn
retreat, so refreshing after the noisy streets of Rome, we
wound our way. What a sudden and sharp change and
contrast we experienced on entering the gateway into the
narrow, picturesque, but most squalid streets — if one may
call them so — of the little huddled-up town. But what
pictures, making us cry aloud for admiration, we caught,
set in frames of archways and galleries, as we passed along,
of the distant meadows and mountains! We soon reached
our destination, the Hotel of the Sibyl, where we were ex-
pected and welcomed, and soon were enabled to *wipe* off the
dust, — for there is something very sticky, almost greasy,
about this Roman dust. While supper was preparing
I hurried out over the great pavement of the kitchen hall
below, through the rear door, and found myself on the
stone terrace of the Temple of the Sibyl, face to face with
that glorious historic amphitheatre. The golden moon —
such it now was — beamed down above the steep moun-
tain opposite upon the luxurious foliage and the silvery
cascades that all around, dimly twinkling, rushed and
roared and plunged down the encircling steep, and were
lost in the gloom and green below. On the extreme left
was evidently the main fall, for there the roar was most
intense and the spray rose like clouds of smoke from a
mighty fire. On my right, where the main fall originally
was before '26, I could discern a bridge and the rugged
outworks of houses, and nearest to me across the chasm,
a walled yard full of goats folded for the night. In the
moonlight gleamed on the stones at the foot of the temple
the linen which always figured in the pictures I had seen
of the Temple of Vesta, as it is also called. How impres-
sive and how sudden a sensation it was to come right from

town and tavern, and stand and look up at that ancient circle of temple columns cut out of the old lava-rock, which had been thrown out and hardened ages ago, when these hollows were craters of volcanoes. The fiery liquid had congealed into this adamantine hardness, while the watery element was still rushing and roaring and tumbling in 'wild torrents fiercely glad.' But I had to go in to supper, which we took in a room decorated with most extraordinary frescos; goat's milk, like cream, in a huge decanter, being one of the most remarkable features of our meal. Then we all went out and stayed on the terrace till ten, lost in reverie and rapture amidst the beauties and glories of that most enchanting scene of art, nature, and history. We scorned and spurned the proposition of a wretch to let on Bengal light for our entertainment. I went to my room, which was directly over the narrow street; but it was hard to sleep, because I had so much of half-seen, half-studied spectacle on my mind.

"Early morning found me again on the temple terrace inspecting in clear daylight what I had only seen in 'the glimpses of the moon.' I was distracted from my contemplation by a precious uproar in the lane below, turning apparently upon a wretched boy's having stolen some wretched bean-pods from a stall. This filled the whole lane with people and eloquent gesticulations and theatrical movements. All the 'Margery Daws' who were shaking their straw beds in the windows over the way, have their heads out at once, and the thing is town talk. The boy is cuffed to and fro, and goes off with a stone in each hand, and stillness is at last restored. We breakfasted at nine, and an hour later were ready to begin our *giro*, or circuit (gyration) round the falls. Passing down through the ambitiously named Piazza di San Giorgio, a sort of stable-yard back of the church, which has been built into or upon the rectangular temple adjoining the Sibyl's, we continued descending through an iron gateway into the winding path which leads by a succession of galleries in the rock and through the woods, down to the bottom of the gorge, — the two chief objects of wonder, and they very wonderful, being the grotto of Neptune and at the very bottom the grotto of the Siren. These are caverns hollowed out by the rush of the waters into a suite (so to speak) of the most enormously grotesque chambers, the roof and sides of which mimic all sorts of creatures in all sorts of contortions, — torsos to which the famous one in the Vatican is a mere trifle, beasts, birds, fishes, turned into stone, and stony suggestions of creatures never named or dreamed. Having reached the bottom on the other side of the ravine, we found our donkeys waiting with their guide, and sundry boys eager to serve as persuaders, punchers, pounders, as the case might require, of those wayward beasts. I consented to let one of them 'pay attention,' as he expressed it, to my steed. And very delicate attention he paid him. It was the first donkey-ride I ever took in my life, and I was somewhat proud of my prowess. I fancied my beast was as intelligent as Balaam's, for every time I said ' Allons donc ! ' he would start and run famously. I did not know that at such times the *hind-officer* always gave the poor animal a hint of my meaning with a sharp stick. Several times I found myself leading the van, and at a smart trot ; and gradually I came to have implicit faith in my long-eared friend, especially as I felt that my open umbrella would serve as a parachute in case of a tumble, no less than a parasol.

"We stopped when we came to a point right above the smoking cataract, and dismounting descended a stairway to the terrace where the double tunnel of nearly one thousand feet in length emerges. It is cut into the flank of the mountain to turn aside the main body of the river. How beautiful it was to stand behind the stream and see it just as it glided over the edge for its tremendous leap, and then to look on the olive stream sweeping on so quietly below between its green banks down through the winding valley !

" We went on again towards a road from which the town began to stand out over against us, as I have oftenest seen it in the photographs. We passed a tank by the roadside under a wall on which the inscription S. P. Q. and (not R., but) J. spoke volumes of history. Before long we were entering into olive woods, and passing the site of a villa came to the extensive ruins of that of Quintilius Varro, a general under Augustus, where the ploughed field under the olives was full of bits of marble and mosaic pavement, and from which we had a commanding view of those ruins across the valley which some call the Villa of Mæcenas, and others the Forum of Tivoli. From hence, too, we beheld the so-called Cascatelle that came rushing down from those ruins by the beautiful patches of garden in a series of ribbon cascades, perhaps the most picturesquely lovely of all the water-works in the neighborhood. Especially beautiful is the effect produced by the appearance of the green moss-topped rocks on which one of the falls breaks, and which look like a cluster of cypress-tops with the water spring-ing over them, their smooth, green, round, heavy plumes making such a lovely contrast to the snowy spray that breaks over them. Crossing the stream again at the foot of the olive hill, we soon wound up the old Roman pave-ment of the Via Tiburtina, and reached the gate of the Villa D' Este, where, finding those of our party who had not joined our excursion, we went in and enjoyed the rich beauties of that quaint and luxurious garden. From its parapet I looked across the Campagna to where the dome of St. Peter's showed solitary and impressive like a rock on the horizon of the ocean. I made my way home alone, and was glad to sit down and cool my eyes in my dark chamber."

Mr. Brooks was fortunate enough to make several interesting literary acquaintances at Rome, besides those already mentioned. One of these was Gregorovius, the eminent German historian of Rome and the papacy. A visit to Severn, the friend of Shelley and Keats, and companion of the latter in his dying hours, he notes with many expressions of pleasure:—

" I could not have conceived that he was an old man. What a fresh, blooming, genial link between the generation of George IV. and our own! I noticed on entering that some of his own pictures hung on the wall ; among others, that of the skeleton ship, with Death on board, appearing to the vessel of the ancient mariner. Also the loveliest portrait of a young woman ; and when we began to rally our friend on his illness, he said, ' Ah, but do you know the cause ? The death of that dear daughter,' pointing to the very picture I had noticed. She had died within the year ; a most promising artist, as are all his children. It was delightful to hear the old gentleman, with his blooming face and sweet eyes, talk about Keats and Shelley and the rest. I was amused when my mention of Hogg's Biography of Shelley, which was stopped in the midst by the family's recalling the materials, started such an earnest appeal to me, as if I possibly might be persuaded to go on and finish it. Margaret Foley smiled. I was too much amazed at the idea to do so. Severn said he had talked with Lady Shelley a good deal about the matter, and knew how glad she would be to have it done. He spoke proudly of his son's progress in art, and of the war in North Italy as already begun, and was very confident that Venice would be wrested from Austria. Cardinal Antonelli in a conversation had expressed the same conviction. He took us into his great room and showed us his pictures, — a truly noble room. The picture of the Marys at the sepulchre, and the angels (female forms) sitting at the head and foot, reached to the ceiling. His female faces are full of sweetness, noble enthusiasm, and tender fire. So is the face of the Magdalen bringing the ointment in that singular picture the 'Passion Flowers.' The picture of the 'Marriage in Cana' he is still at work on. We asked Severn whether it was true, as we had heard (on his alleged authority), that Keats did *not* utter the words 'Here lies one whose name was written in water,' etc. He replied, that Keats did breathe the very wish and words with his last breath, only he (Severn) thought it was time the old question and quarrel ceased to be perpetuated, and he was wishing to have a monument erected by subscription in place of the present stone. He spoke with emphatic and enthusiastic love of the Fields, and said he had prepared a sketch of Shelley for the 'Atlantic.'"

Mr. Brooks also did a deal of reading at odd hours, mostly on subjects connected with Rome and Roman life. He read for the first time the charming plays of Goldoni, and attended the open-air theatre improvised between the walls of the Mausoleum of Augustus. He wandered about the streets at all hours, studying the people, and once at least had a narrow escape from robbery, if not violence, in a dangerous quarter of the city, into which he had unwittingly strayed. But the sight of that peaceful face, with its mild blue eyes, seems to have disarmed the populace that had ominously closed in about him ; and he went his way unmolested, to the thankful surprise of his good landlady, to whom he afterward related the adventure. He hears his first nightingale, sees his first lark upsoaring to the skies, and plucks his first orange with his own hands in the Barberini Gardens, — three experiences well worth chronicling by a poet. Meanwhile letters from home bring messages of comfort and love, and from Vienna Count Auersperg (the poet Anastasius Grün) writes welcoming him back to Germany.

Rome was still under papal rule, and Holy Week was celebrated in old-time splendor and pageantry, which he describes at considerable length in his journal. Sunday, April 1, he writes : —

" The bells began to make a glad uproar soon after midnight, and the cannon roared and bellowed from St. Angelo very early, making long reverberations in the surrounding hills, so that one (that is, I) did not get a continuous sleep for an hour together the whole night. The morning looked a little ominous, but the day proved pleasant. At nine I went round for the Longfellows, and we took a carriage to St. Peter's, where we found that the Pope had already entered the church, and was just finishing his devotions at the Chapel of the Holy Sacrament. By the time we were opposite that spot, we saw the peacock's feathers and the canopy ; and almost at that moment the old man was lifted up and borne forward, looking to my eye very like a chalk-drawing on the air, so pale and faint he seemed as he threw out his blessing. They bore him up to the tribune, while the trumpets blew a sublime strain from a balcony over the central door of the church. They deposited him somewhere, and a grand music began and continued over an hour, with slight intervals. It was majestic and stirring, even though we could hear only the sound ; but it was not so grand as the music of the illimitable ocean, of which the footfalls of the myriads that crowded the church reminded one. I never so wished that great unmeaning baldachin and that little black St. Peter in the white marble chair away as I did this morning; nor did I ever feel so much the injury done to the effect of the church by so much action and attitudinizing of the statues. In fact, I wished the whole of these ornaments away for a moment, to see what would be the effect of the grand space and proportions of the edifice. One thing gave me a new impression of the enormous size of the building. I wondered what a certain something that looked like a bird-cage was up against the cornice, and found it was a scaffolding for workmen. Whole villages of country people — shock-headed peasant boys, with great hobnailed shoes and laced leather leggings ; men looking as if they had grown into the nature of the region they inhabited, — rough, hirsute, rocky, ragged ; women whose haggard visages contrasted singularly with their gay attire — came in and went out, and were no more than a drop in the bucket. The Swiss Guard looked more like harlequins than ever to-day, as they glided to and fro in the throng. On the whole, I found the affair somewhat heavy. But when the time came for the elevation of the Host, and the files of soldiers lining the broad avenue through the length of the church sank on their knees, and then that tender, soul-thrilling peal of the silver trumpets woke the silence, there was something worth all the waiting for, — something, as the books say, never to be forgotten. When it ended I went out into the crowd that already seemed to fill the great square, although other crowds were to be emptied into it from that monster church. What a sight, — that motley mass of natives and strangers, city fashionables and coun-

try folk in all their odd costumes ; soldiery by thousands,
on horse and on foot ; the roofs of the great colonnades
black with people ; the windows and balconies of the
farthest houses full of heads ; the steps of the church
crowded with people gazing out on the scene ! Fortu-
nately the sky was slightly overcast, and a cooling breeze
stirred. It was about half past eleven when I came out.
At twelve the cannon fired, then two smaller bells were
rung, and the great one struck in the balcony under the
southern clock. The singers, who till then had occupied
the great central balcony over which the crimson canopy
hung, and below which floated the crimson cloth of Clem-
ent XI., withdrew ; and the cardinals, in those ridiculous-
looking white mitres, came successively to the front and
filed round, apparently making obeisance to the Pope, and
laying off their tall head-pieces to replace them with red
skull-caps. The bells now ceased, and a chant began in
behind the balcony, — apparently a part of the blessing, a
sort of preamble. Then the old Pope arose, and flung his
voice and his hands aloft with wonderful vigor for an old
man of seventy-five ; and in three minutes the blessing was
over, and the air rang with shouts of ' *Viva, evviva !* ' not
only to the Pope, but (if I caught it rightly) even to Peter
and Paul and other apostles, the country people around me
cheering vociferously. Some official then thrust down
printed copies of a plenary indulgence ; and the eagerness
of the crowd to secure them was partly amusing and partly
alarming, as they moved backward on the steps with up-
turned faces, flinging up their arms at the risk of tumbling
over backward. And now began the slow, laborious process
of getting away, — that enormous crowd having to squeeze
out through two narrow lanes, and still more narrowly over
the Bridge of St. Angelo through a way choked up with
carriages ; but I, by my natural slenderness and acquired

dexterity, contrived to zig-zag about through the line of vehicles and platoons of people so as to reach home with my share of the Pope's blessing soon after two o'clock.

"At seven o'clock in the evening we quietly went forth to the Piazza of Trinita Monti ; and, lo ! as we emerged upon the place, there stood the indescribably beautiful illumination of St. Peter's ; and glad we were, after all, that we had not seen the process of lighting up, and that the finished thing gleamed at once all complete before us across the valley in silvery softness. Words fail even to hint the enchanting loveliness of this fairy-like creation. It seemed as if the old St. Peter's had gone, and this light, jewel-work imitation in silver fire had sprung up by magic in its place. It looked not like a thing of this earth, but like something conjured there by spirits. Somebody said it was a piece of the New Jerusalem, come down from heaven. A dark-blue cloud, stretching across the western sky, made for it a glorious background. We went up into the balcony of the sculptor Mozier, in that high house directly over the Spanish staircase, bearing on its front the inscription, ' Purior hic aër, hic late aspectus in urbem' ('Here is a purer air, here a wide prospect over the city'). We found there a large assemblage of people, — among others, Madame Rutka, the sister of Kossuth. There was also a young lady from Chicago, most eloquent in her eulogy of Martineau, together with many artists. We waited and watched for the famous moment when the silver illumination changes suddenly to a golden one. A little before eight we remarked a peculiar darting to and fro of lights in behind the rows of lamps, and presently a red flame darted at the cross and took possession of it ; and from thence it seemed to fly down all over the building, till the whole was sparkling and blazing and flashing with golden fire. The restless glitter gradually subsided into a

more steady glow ; but all the evening a beautiful waving
continued along the gleaming rows of rich, golden lights.
It was hard to say whether the golden or the silver illu-
mination was the more beautiful.  Both were perfect in
their way ; and Nature might have reason to fear their
rivalry, were it not that Nature itself contributed so much
to the result."

The increasing heat and gradual lessening of the
American and English colony induced him to leave
the Eternal City.  It had become so endeared to him
that he viewed his approaching departure with real
sorrow, feeling that he should never revisit it again.
To his homesickness was now added what he calls
*Rome*-sickness.  But the war-clouds in the North in-
stead of lifting grew deeper and deeper; and so, on
June 14, he bade farewell to all the glory and charm
of Rome, and in company with the artist Freeman and
his family, departed for Florence, visiting on the way
Terni, Foligno, and Perugia.

Arriving in Florence on the 16th, he found a lodg-
ing at Casa Guidi, from whose windows Mrs. E. B.
Browning heard the child singing " Bella Liberta,"
and to whose walls is affixed a memorial tablet to that
noble poetess and woman.  One of his first visits was
to the little Protestant cemetery where she lies buried,
together with Arthur Hugh Clough, Theodore Par-
ker, Walter Savage Landor, and other kindred dust.
He receives a cordial welcome from Minister Marsh
and Professor Botta, and finds much to enjoy at
Firenze la Bella.  While he is abiding there, war is
officially declared by Italy against Austria, and he

witnesses the departure of King Victor Emmanuel
at the head of his army to undertake the recapture of
Venice.   He visits the Italian Parliament, attending
its last session, — a scene of great confusion and noise.
Everywhere the tricolor is waving, and the popular
enthusiasm kindles his own spirit.   But he is "natu-
rally such a peace man" that he takes the less in-
terest in the stirring events which now are agitating
Europe to the core.

"I thought this morning, as I heard the man crying the
newspapers, 'L' Opinione,' 'Il Popolo,' 'L' Italie,' how dif-
ferently things go on in regard to the war from what they
did with us.   For instance, two weeks have gone since that
first battle, and yet there has come no published list of killed
and wounded.   One single day our two girls were making
lint in the house, but in general how little stir there seems
to be compared with what our war made !   However, war is
a more normal thing in this part of the world."

On July 3 he left Florence, and after a short stay
at Bologna and Milan, meeting everywhere soldiery,
transport-trains, and earthworks, he proceeded by way
of Como and Splügen over the Via Mala to Switzer-
land.   July 9 he is at Zurich, and thence travelled
on to Lucerne and the Rhigi.   It was with peculiar in-
terest that the translator of Schiller's "William Tell"
visited the traditional scene of that hero's exploits.
He was constantly meeting friends, — Parke Godwin
and wife, George Ripley, and at Professor Kapp's
in Zurich Mr. Villard with his wife, a daughter of
William Lloyd Garrison.   Brienz, Interlaken, Lau-
terbrunnen, Thun, Berne, Basel, and the intervening

places of interest were visited in turn, and his diary overflows with admiration and delight at the beauty and grandeur of Alpine scenery. At Munich he finds Bodenstedt, the learned and genial author of Mirza Schaffy's poems and other works of value. Geibel is not in town, but he meets the writer Herman Ling, Professor Fichte, son of the philosopher Fichte, and Ernst Forster, the historian of art, and who had been the husband of Jean Paul Richter's daughter. The white-haired veteran in literature greeted most heartily the translator of " Titan " and " Hesperus," and showed him interesting relics of Richter.

On August 17 Mr. Brooks passed through Salzburg and the Tyrol on his way to Vienna. War had now been declared between Prussia and the South German States, and everywhere he encountered soldiers and military preparations. Minister Motley, his college mate, pleasantly received him, and Vienna proved a place of varied interest. He witnessed a performance of Goethe's "Faust" at the Hof Theater, and goes into raptures over it. To his sincere regret Count von Auersperg was absent on his estates ; and hence these two friends, while constantly corresponding, never met on earth. Everywhere Mr. Brooks unexpectedly came upon persons who knew him as the translator of German masterpieces, and delighted to show him honor. At Stuttgart this is especially the case. Here resides his fellow poet, correspondent, and friend, Platinius, a zealous advocate of America, who introduces him to various eminent persons, — Baron Cotta, the painter Wagner, and others.

On the 27th of August occurs "the memorable evening" in Mr. Brooks's literary career, when a company of authors and poets assembled to show their regard for the amiable and accomplished translator of "Faust" and "Titan." Among those present were Dr. Gerok, the renowned preacher and poet, Jacob Corvinus, a son of the poet Gustav Schwab, Dr. Eduard Hoefer, a favorite poet, his friend Platinius, and others. He is introduced at the close of the social meal as one to whom Germany is much indebted, whereupon the whole company rise and drink his health with great enthusiasm. This was the culmination of all the kindnesses he had received, and Mr. Brooks left Stuttgart with a grateful heart. Nuremberg he finds full of Prussian soldiers waiting till the indemnity should be paid. He is a firm believer in German unity under Prussia's leadership, but the atmosphere of war is oppressive to him and he hurries away.

At Leipzig he revisits, with his Newport friend the pianist James Wilson, the Knauth family, whose beautiful German home-life he so much admired. Soldiers abound wherever he turns, and the cholera is reported as again threatening. But he is eager to get to Weimar, whither he carries a letter of introduction to Walther von Goethe, the grandson of the poet, from Freiligrath. He is most cordially received, and has several hours with him in "free and friendly chat," — the Baron speaking English with uncommon fluency, and proving to be a most cultivated and agreeable person. He shows him about the house and

haunts of the great poet, and makes his second visit
to Weimar a most enjoyable one.  At Eisenach, a city
identified with Luther's career, where we find Mr.
Brooks on the 8th of September, he relates that the
guide who takes him over the Wartburg has never
heard of Wittenberg !  A glorious day on the Rhine,
an hour of solemn silence amid the shadows of Co-
logne Cathedral, and he bids farewell forever to beloved
Germany, in which he seems to have enjoyed every-
thing but the soldiers and the cooking.  September 14
he is in London again, having rounded the circle of
Europe in a year's time.  On Sunday he preached for
Conway at the South Place Chapel.  He paid a parting
visit to Freiligrath, Russell Sturgis, and other friends,
and passed "a memorable day" at Stratford-on-Avon,
meeting the Rev. William H. Channing.  Thence he
made a flying trip to Edinburgh, where he was en-
tertained by Prof. William Smith, the translator
of Fichte, and there on Sunday preached a second
time.  In Glasgow he made the acquaintance of Pro-
fessor Nichol, and after a journey through the Tro-
sachs returned and sailed for his native country on
the steamer "Asia," Sept. 29, 1866, bringing back
with him five boxes of literary and other treasures,
and a heart filled with grateful memories that were
his solace and delight during the remaining years of
his life.  At sea he "composed" himself "by making
rhymes."  October 9 they reached Halifax, and he
is "rejoiced to hear the news of the American elec-
tions, and that the land is once more saved."  Twelve
days later he arrives in Newport, and is warmly

greeted by a social gathering of his parishioners and
friends, at which the Rev. Mr. Webster, his substi-
tute while abroad, and Col. T. W. Higginson make
addresses, and Mrs. Julia Ward Howe and Henry
T. Tuckerman read poems of welcome.

Mr. Brooks returned from Europe much refreshed
in body and mind, and with a store of new informa-
tion and happy memories which through years to
come brightened his discourse and was an unfailing
source of enjoyment to him.  His pulpit labors were
resumed, and showed the enlargement of mind and
recuperation of energies which his recent experiences
had yielded him.  With increased ardor he threw
himself into his literary work and especially his Ger-
man studies.  Besides review articles and occasional
poems he now prepared an elaborate series of lectures
on Rome, which displayed not only a lively fancy
and much descriptive power, but no little erudition.
The poems, serious and humorous, which he had
written for the edification of friends while in the
Eternal City, were now collected in a little pamphlet,
and printed under the title "Roman Rhymes," for
the benefit of the annual church fair.  A work of
more pretentious character was his version of Leo-
pold Schefer's "Laien Brevier," or "Layman's Bre-
viary," published in 1867, which was followed in 1873
by another and similar work of the same author,
"The World Priest."  These volumes contain the
moralizing in poetical form of a writer very popular
in Germany; and Mr. Brooks was, as usual, highly
successful in rendering into English the thought and

idiomatic turns of the original. In the mean time he was again engaged earnestly in translating the great work of Friedrich Rückert, "The Wisdom of the Brahmin."

Although Mr. Brooks was naturally disinclined to practical affairs, and by his gentle, peace-loving disposition especially unfitted for engaging in any aggressive movement, yet we find him deeply interested in the various attempts at organization and missionary activity which in later years have characterized the denomination to which he belonged. In the year 1865 the Unitarians formed a National Conference of churches, adopting as their basis of union a series of articles whose preamble called upon "all disciples of the Lord Jesus Christ" to unite in the "service of God and the building up of the kingdom of his Son." This phraseology, while it undoubtedly expressed the theological attitude of the large majority of the Conference, was strenuously resisted by a numerically small but intellectually and morally important minority of the body. Under the leadership of Francis E. Abbott, Octavius B. Frothingham, William J. Potter, and others, an earnest effort was made so to amend the preamble as to do away with its acknowledgment of the supreme and exceptional authority of Jesus Christ. This attempt was as earnestly resisted by Drs. H. W. Bellows, A. P. Putnam, the Rev. George H. Hepworth, and the great preponderance of delegates. In the excited discussions to which this issue led at this and subsequent conferences, Mr. Brooks, with many others, assumed a broad and reconciling

position.  His own loyalty to the personal character
and historic claims of Jesus Christ was complete and
unquestioned, but it was accompanied by a breadth
of sympathy, an insistence on the spirit rather than
the letter of religion, which were worthy of his Tran-
scendental faith, the commission he had received
from Dr. Channing, and the teachings of the great
Germans whose writings had been his favorite and en-
thusiastic study.  In 1870 the Unitarian Conference
held a stormy session in the city of New York.  The
radical demand for a modification of the existing
articles was met by a counter-demand on the part
of the more orthodox delegates for a definite and
fixed creed, or statement of Unitarian principles.
These two movements neutralized each other, and
neither was successful, the Conference practically re-
affirming its original position.  This led to the
withdrawal of the more extreme members from the
organization.  Mr. Brooks deeply deplored this, and
on his return preached a sermon to his people in
which he gave them his impressions of the meeting,
and which breathes the most catholic and progressive
spirit.  After speaking warmly of Dr. Eliot's sermon,
he says that he yet felt that it did not reach the
main issue.  Speaking of certain brethren who could
not call themselves Christian, yet desired to work with
the Conference in its general aims and methods, he
says : —

"I confess that I felt a deal of sympathy for these
brethren, — call their consciences weak, morbid, or foolishly
fastidious if you will.  It seemed to me that if a single

soul stood waiting and willing and longing to work with us and to believe with us, but felt itself by our definitions excluded or not heartily welcomed, here was precisely a case for the application of Paul's noble words, ' Him that is weak in the faith receive ye, but not to doubtful disputations.' It seemed to me that one conscience is of more account than all imposing shows of unanimity in the statement of a creed."

This appeared to him the true interior spirit of Unitarianism and of Christianity. Such was also, we know, the opinion held by that master mind Dr. Orville Dewey, as from his country retreat he watched the struggles and transformations his religious fellowship was undergoing. The intense party spirit of that day has largely died out. The issue, though still disturbing the Unitarian body, has ceased to be an all-absorbing topic in its discussions, and will doubtless before long be finally disposed of in the spirit of freedom, justice, and peace. But honor is due to those fathers of the Liberal Church who, like Dr. Orville Dewey and Charles T. Brooks, — the logician and the poet, — from the very beginning pierced to the heart of the controversy, and pointed out those principles of intellectual liberty, — respect for the individual conscience, and an inclusive sympathy which alone can lead to its righteous and permanent solution.

A new and severer trial than any with which he had been visited was now impending. His eyes had long been giving him much trouble, caused in great part by the vast amount of literary labor which he performed, and which often extended deep into the night. Soon he was almost entirely blind. By the advice of his physicians he entered the Carney Hospital at South Boston, where he remained for some months. He quite charmed his nurses and all with whom he came in contact by the singular patience and sweetness with which he bore his affliction, and the calm courage he opposed to the painful operation which he was compelled to undergo. The Rev. Dr. Bartol relates: " One of his nurses, a sister at the hospital, when I said to her, ' He is a good man,' replied, ' He is a little child.' This is testimony from Rome. No pope could better it. It covered and stilled my praise." The result of the operation was in so far successful that Mr. Brooks returned to Newport with the partial sight of one of his eyes. Henceforth he was compelled to use a powerful magnifier in the spectacles he had worn for so long a period that his friends can scarcely recall him without them.

Mr Brooks returned to his post of duty; but it became evident that his increasing years and infirmities would not allow him long to continue his pastoral relation. His pulpit service came to an end, to the mutual regret of minister and people, on the last Sunday before Thanksgiving, 1871, when he preached his farewell sermon. A few weeks previously his home had been brightened by the marriage of his youngest daughter, Elizabeth, to Lieut. Washburn Maynard, son of the late Hon. Horace Maynard, of Tennessee. Mr. Brooks's retirement from active

service in the ministry was facilitated by a bequest
made him in 1869 by his noble friend the late
James Arnold, of New Bedford, who was found on
his death to have generously remembered certain of
his clerical acquaintances in his will. Other friends
of Mr. Brooks now stepped in with their offerings
of affection, determined that he who had done so
much to make other people's lives happy should
spend his remaining years free from worldly care,
in a contented and beautiful old age. His daughter
Harriet, early left a widow, returned to Newport
with her children, to whom he was greatly attached,
and made for her parents a delightful home. The
parish could not bear to sunder entirely his pastoral
relation with them, and it was not until the spring
of 1873 that his resignation was accepted.

A letter dated March 6, 1873, abounding in as-
surances of grateful affection, was drawn up by the
church, and forwarded to Mr. Brooks. Thus closed a
pastorate which had extended over a third of a cen-
tury, and had been fruitful in labors for righteousness
and piety.

Now began the closing and most beautiful chapter
in the life of Charles T. Brooks, — a happy, benig-
nant old age, free from worldly care and ambition.
The beloved centre, with his wife, of the household,
surrounded with dutiful and affectionate children and
grandchildren and the old-time friends in whom his
heart delighted, his days were passed in " the quiet
and still air of delightful studies," and occupied with
" happy, idle labors," which afforded him congenial

employment and the grateful sense of still being
useful to the world.  Withdrawn from public duties,
he was able to devote himself the more completely to
his favorite literary pursuits.  It was truly wonder-
ful how much his facile and industrious pen was able
to achieve in this field, notwithstanding his impaired
eyesight.  The calls upon him for occasional poems,
hymns, translations, etc., were incessant.  His advice
and good offices were sought by literary aspirants and
dilettanti, and rarely refused.  Many articles in prose
and verse contributed to the periodical press of his
day, a long series of rhymes and riddles written for
children, scores of Carriers' New Year's addresses fur-
nished the newspapers of Salem and Newport, and a
series of published works bore witness to his tireless
activity.  It was a favorite pastime with Mr. Brooks
to cut out the comic pictures of the well-known
Munich " Bilderbogen," and paste them in order into
little books of his own making, writing beneath each
picture a rhymed translation of the German text.
Hundreds of such little books were prepared by
him for the annual fairs of his society, where they
afforded much amusement for young and old.  Simi-
lar in nature were the English versions of M. Busch's
grotesque children's books, which he published at va-
rious times during these later years.  As his contri-
bution to its fortieth anniversary, he printed in 1875
a brief " History of the Unitarian Church in New-
port."  One significant passage from this little work
deserves to be quoted here, as furnishing food for
thought : —

"It would seem strange, if we did not know how commonly vague and secondary meanings attach themselves to human language, to find a body already incorporated as a 'Unitarian Congregational *Church*,' and assembling in a house called a *church*, voting to have a *church* formed among them. Does it not sound a little like a *body's* asking to have the *soul* put into it? One would suppose that to a body of Liberal Christians the service of praise and prayer, in which the congregation is expected to partake, would be as sacred as the commemorative service of the sacrament. The fact that only such a mere handful could be induced to join in the latter observance shows, I think, that we are still in the shadow of the old superstition, either in the people's understanding of the subject or else in the Church's own manner of observing the communion service. I think probably we are behind the age and the Christian ideal in both respects. Nothing has been a greater damper to my own heartiness in the communion service, and nothing have I labored more earnestly to do away, than the idea in the popular mind that a Christian congregation and a Christian church are two things, — an idea producing an *obliquity* and doubleness of spiritual vision regarding Christianity, seriously hindering, it seems to me, the growth of a religious society."

A series of translations of Berthold Auerbach's novels led to a correspondence in which the less amiable traits of that eminent author were displayed. A communication and poem, "Flood Ireson," which appeared in the Boston "Transcript" for Feb. 22, 1877, won deserved praise. Among others Dr. O. W. Holmes wrote him, commending its "truthful tenderness," and the evidence it brought for a different and higher estimate of the skipper of Marblehead, and

7

expressed the hope that it might be read side by side with Whittier's famous ballad.  But the most notable literary fruit of these closing years was the completion of his translation of Friedrich Rückert's great poem, " The Wisdom of the Brahmin," of which the first six books were published in 1882, the remaining two volumes of his version being still in manuscript.  This poem is one of the great masterpieces of German literature, and its transfer into English was perhaps the most considerable literary undertaking of Mr. Brooks.  The task was one of surpassing difficulty.  The sententious wisdom, the mystical senses half disclosed in the original, the continual play on words, the curiously elaborate and involved construction, the Eastern imagery and atmosphere in which Rückert's imagination revelled, were all reproduced with remarkable fidelity and skill.  Had this version been published half a century since, when the Transcendental philosophy was uppermost in New England, it could not have failed to make a profound impression.  As it is, a lessened sympathy with its intellectual standpoint and the appearance of more popular presentations of the thought and poetry of the Orient, like Edwin Arnold's "Light of Asia," have prevented Rückert's great poem from arriving at any large acceptance among us.  Perhaps its day is yet to come, and the publication of the remaining volumes will then be called for.  In any case, it is pleasant to reflect that the closing literary labors of our friend should have produced the noblest intellectual fruit of his life.

Although withdrawn from the active ministry
and never again preaching a sermon, Mr. Brooks
continued to take a deep interest in the affairs of
his former church. The society had called as his
successor the Rev. John C. Kimball, for whose abili-
ties and earnestness of character Mr. Brooks enter-
tained a high regard, and with whom he remained
in kindliest relations throughout his brief ministry.
The congregation still looked upon Mr. Brooks as
their pastor emeritus. Many were the calls made
upon him for counsel and sympathy, and his visits
on the sick and sorrowing went on much as before
his resignation. No parish gathering seemed com-
plete without his gentle, genial presence. Mean-
while he was the most loyal supporter and friend
of the minister in the pulpit, who, looking down on
Sunday into the attentive, rapt face of the venerated
man, — his most appreciative hearer and mildest
critic, — felt his discourse lifted with new enthu-
siasm and his appeals for the good life pointed with
a more personal and convincing illustration. But it
was on the sad and glad occasions in the domestic
life of his friends that Mr. Brooks's presence and
word were most sought. An interesting occurrence
of this kind was his solemnization at Newport in
1878 of the marriage service which united his friend
the French sculptor Bartholdi, designer of the colos-
sal statue "Liberty enlightening the World," to the
woman of his choice. The funeral services of his
former parishioners he considered it to the last a
sacred duty to attend, and often his discourse or

prayer brought consolation to sorrowing hearts. It was his custom, observed through long years and with entire impartiality, to read on such occasions some original lines expressive of the prevailing sentiment. None of his poetic effusions, perhaps, won him such deep and lasting gratitude as these commemorative verses. They are treasured in many homes to-day as memorials both of their loved and lost and of the saintly man who wrote them. The death of his dear friends Margaret Foley and his classmate Augustus Story, he commemorated with touching tributes which appeared in print. Sorrow invaded his own home when his first-born, Charles Mason Brooks, returned to Newport to die, passing away after a lingering illness on the 24th of July, 1881.

On the streets of Newport Mr. Brooks was a well-known and beloved figure. As he took his daily walk to the post-office, moving with slow and measured step, because of his imperfect eyesight and a difficulty in breathing which in later life beset him, many were the affectionate looks and greetings which he encountered. He was deeply interested in the public schools of the city, for twenty years serving as a member of the school board. Another cherished institution with him was the Redwood Library, of which he was for a long period a director, and at the time of his death the vice-president. At the sessions of the Town and Country Club — an informal gathering of bright people, summer habitués of Newport, for literary and social culture — Mr. Brooks was a central figure; and his genial, witty presence added much to the interest of the meetings. The annual reunion of the Class of 1832 was an event looked forward to with unflagging eagerness; and no one contributed so much, by reminiscence, poetic effusion, and good fellowship, to keep alive its fast-waning traditions.

When the Harvard Club of Rhode Island was formed, Mr. Brooks entered heartily into the plans of its projectors, and was spared to be present and read a poem at its first meeting in 1882. A pleasant change was brought into his life by the annual visits he continued to make to the winter homes of his friends, and especially to his beloved birthplace, Salem.

There was one trait in Mr. Brooks's character which deserves a special reference, and that is his unbounded sympathy and benevolence towards those in distress. He seemed to be constitutionally unable to refuse any call upon his time or his purse. No doubt he was at times greatly imposed upon by deceitful and impudent applicants for aid. Yet he always affirmed that he was exceptionally blessed in his giving. It was especially persons of foreign birth who were led to seek his sympathy and help because of his acquaintance with their language and well-known relations with foreign literature. During the summer months, especially, a constant succession of Germans, French, Italians, and other foreigners came to seek his counsel and secure his mediation with the more wealthy and charitable cottagers of

Newport. Unappreciated artists, impecunious authors, teachers with a new system but never a pupil, needy and plausible adventurers, eminent and condescending political refugees, hair-brained social philosophers, — to all alike Mr. Brooks listened with infinite patience, and spent his strength and substance in their behalf. In a single instance only was he known to flinch and evade this obligation, when two noble Poles whom he had befriended would insist, in the exuberance of their gratitude, on kneeling and effusively kissing the hands of their benefactor. This was too much for the latter's humility; and whenever this worthy pair hove in sight and bore down upon the parsonage, Mr. Brooks, seizing his hat, would flee into the barn and engage in his favorite exercise of wood-chopping in order to escape his tormentors.

One more duty was now laid upon Mr. Brooks, and one in which he delighted, — to participate in the celebrations with which in 1880 the one hundredth anniversary of the birth of Dr. William Ellery Channing was commemorated by his admirers throughout the civilized world. He prepared and published a brief Memoir of Dr. Channing, which contained also his personal recollections of that eminent man. Of his poem on Channing read on the ninety-ninth anniversary of his birth, in the Unitarian Church at Newport, the Rev. Dr. F. H. Hedge well says that it is replete with profound feeling and fully charged with the inspiration of the theme.

It was decided to build a Channing Memorial

Church in Newport, the city of his birth. With ardor Mr. Brooks seconded the plans of the Rev. Mr. Schermerhorn, the new pastor of the Unitarian Society. By personal appeals, by newspaper and private correspondence, and in other ways he contributed largely to the success of this enterprise. From day to day he watched the building of the new edifice. When at last it was completed, and the beautiful structure was crowded with a grateful congregation, and dedicated with imposing services to the ideals and uses of Liberal Christianity, how it increased the thankfulness and joy of the people to behold among them this saintly man, whose thirty-seven years of faithful ministry had made possible this hour of triumph and congratulation, and to whom the Channing Memorial Church will ever remain a monument, as truly as to the great man whose name is graven on its fore-front.

He was not long to survive this crowning event in his career. The writer of this memoir, who had known and revered Mr. Brooks since childhood, came to Newport as the new pastor of the church. How little did he dream when as a boy he loved to visit the Brooks household, and in after years formed a personal friendship with the gentle poet-preacher, that in the days to come he should be his successor in the Newport pulpit, conduct with sorrowing heart the farewell services at his grave, and write these words in commemoration of his fatherly friend. So mysterious are the counsels of God, so wonderful the providences of the Eternal!

This attachment between the senior and junior
pastor was deepened by a common interest in the Ger-
man language and literature, which came to the one
through parentage and a mother's instruction, and
which Mr. Brooks had acquired by earnest and de-
voted study. But this delightful companionship lasted
barely a year. Mr. Brooks's last literary labor was
to correct the proof-sheets of his translation of Jean
Paul Richter's "Invisible Lodge," a youthful work of
that great author, " a dreamy extravaganza in which
he has embedded a wealth of quaint and abstruse
fancy." We little thought, as we looked over the
proof-sheets together, how soon the gates of the In-
visible Lodge above would open to receive the elder
of the two friends into higher realms of faith and
service.

As his seventieth birthday approached, the church
and Sunday-school made arrangements to give him a
pleasant surprise by celebrating the anniversary with
appropriate exercises and expressions of their regard.
Congratulatory letters had been received from various
friends from abroad, and others had promised their
presence. But it was not to be. What proved to be
his last illness supervened. A complication of ail-
ments and the burden of his increasing years caused
him to sink rapidly. In the last interview which the
writer had with him, he was calm and happy, and
even manifested something of his usual humor. Gen-
tly, peacefully, with little struggle, he passed away on
the tenth day of June, 1883, a few days before the
seventieth anniversary of his birth; and his pure and

amiable spirit ascended to those mansions of light to which he had so often pointed the hopes of his sorrowing friends.

The universal and profound grief caused by the announcement of his death was a beautiful testimony to the affectionate regard which his life and character had awakened in his fellow-men. It is the simple truth to say that no man ever lived in Newport who was so generally esteemed and loved as Charles Timothy Brooks. A large concourse of mourning friends crowded the Channing Church and lined the walk outside on the following Sunday morning, when his funeral took place. Beautiful floral tributes adorned the sanctuary, where for an hour his dust reposed ere it was laid away in the faithful tomb. The services were conducted according to a printed order, the hymns sung having been selected from those of his own writing. The choir sang his favorite anthems, " Rest in the Lord," and " The Lord is mindful of his own." The suddenness of the event and the choice of a Sunday for his burial prevented his clerical friends from attending as they would have desired. But many who were detained at home by parish duty or infirmities sent tender tributes to his memory which were read at the service. Among these were the Rev. Drs. Hedge, Bartol, Clarke, Farley, Furness, the Revs. Rufus Ellis and Augustus Woodbury, his classmates the Rev. Samuel Longfellow and John S. Dwight, Julia Ward Howe, and Oliver Wendell Holmes. A poetic tribute was also read at the service by ex-Governor C. C. Van

Zandt, of Rhode Island. The commemorative ad-
dress by the pastor, phonographically reported, to-
gether with a report of the exercises and transcripts
of the letters read, was published in the "Christian
Register" for June 21, 1883. At the close of the
service hundreds came forward to look once more on
the face of their deceased minister and friend. The
pall-bearers, consisting of the Rev. Dr. Thacher
Thayer, — the venerable ex-pastor of the Orthodox
Congregational Church at Newport, and a long-time
friend of Mr. Brooks, — William K. Covell, John
G. Weaver, the Hon. George Bancroft, George W.
Wales, Elbert J. Anderson, Edmund Tweedy, George
H. Calvert, and Henry C. Stevens, bore him forth
from the church he loved so well. One who was
present reports: —

"During the services there was a heavy shower, with
thunder ; but by the time the vast audience had taken their
farewell look of the beloved face, the clouds lifted, and blue
sky and a cheering sun looked down on the long procession
that wound slowly through the narrow streets to the last
resting-place. The exercises at the grave were very brief,
but instinct with hope and trust.

"Then the dust was committed to the dust, and the lover
of Nature was left to the keeping of the beautiful June.
As the last carriage turned down the pathetically named
Farewell Street, a song-sparrow with a burst of sweet
melody flew over the sleeping singer and disappeared in
the sky above."

Tributes of personal esteem and acknowledgment
of Mr. Brooks's literary services appeared in the

Providence Journal, Newport News, Newport Mercury, the Boston Transcript, Boston Advertiser, New York Tribune, New York Times, New York Herald, Harper's Weekly, Chicago Unity, Salem Gazette, and many other papers. The Newport Historical Society, the Redwood Library Directors, and the Channing Memorial Church Trustees passed resolutions of respect and regard for his memory. The first session of the Town and Country Club, on July 16, was devoted to addresses upon his personal virtues and literary labors by the President, Mrs. Julia Ward Howe, the Rev. Dr. James Freeman Clarke, Samuel Powell, Esq., and others. On the 17th of December ensuing, the Essex Institute of Salem, Mass., of which Mr. Brooks had been a valued member, held a commemorative meeting, at which his classmate Dr. Henry Wheatland presided; and papers on his Salem and Newport life were read by the Revs. E. B. Willson and Charles W. Wendté, respectively. Communications were also received from Robert S. Rantoul and William P. Andrews, of Salem. These proceedings were afterward printed in the Historical Collections of the Essex Institute. A number of poetical tributes were also offered in memory of the dead poet by the Rev. William Silsbee, Christopher P. Cranch, W. P. Andrews, Martha P. Lowe, Lydia L. A. Very, S. D. Robbins, Edward F. Hayward, James D. Waters, and others. We can insert but one of these, by his classmate and intimate friend John S. Dwight. It was read at the next annual reunion of the Class of 1832 after Mr. Brooks's death.

## C. T. B.

Not here! not yet?   Where lingers our dear poet?
   Scanning each other's faces, sit we dumb
And wait for *him*, while in our hearts we know it —
      He will not come.

At every call that summoned us as brothers,
   In quick response, whole-hearted, up he sprang;
Not listening for the tardier note of others,
      His bugle rang.

Without the door his voice leapt in before him,
   (Returning Spring ne'er came more cheerily!)
For of the love which, one and all, we bore him,
      Full sure was he.

How blithe his coming! fragrant armfuls bringing,
   Fresh wreaths of song, which at our feet he flung,
Setting the echoes of the rich days ringing
      When we were young!

How radiant he was! how clear and truthful!
   That face bespoke a heart that knew no guile;
The step, the glance, the voice, were still so youthful,
      So sweet the smile!

For he was childlike, innocent, and holy;
   His law was duty, and his labor love:
True friend alike to all, or high or lowly,
      All pride above.

In simple faith, for living waters thirsting,
   Life's wondrous labyrinth he bravely trod;
The hand unseen, that led him, fondly trusting,
      He walked with God.

And as he walked, his eyes, with rapture beaming,
  Saw beauty, Deity, in all around ;
His soul, with happy thoughts and fancies teeming,
    Sought more, and found.

And so in him Apollo and the Muses
  Bathed the fine faculties, kept *will* alive,
Sent fruitful hours, which Fate to them refuses
    Who faintly strive.

Those fruits on us he lavished without measure,
  How many, many well-remembered times!
How all he felt or thought about with pleasure
    Still ran in rhymes!

When darkness came he failed not, never losing
  "The vision and the faculty divine,"
From Song's far founts still lovingly transfusing
    The costly wine.

In short'ning days of golden-ripe October,
  The lingering leaves their warmer colors wear ;
His ripeness took a hue both rich and sober,
    Yet passing fair!

Our Spring's a dream; but there's an Indian summer, —
  Of well-kept faith the mellow aftermath, —
Whereof life's raw recruit and gay new-comer
    No inkling hath.

*He* knew it well, our saint, but now translated,
  Ripe for the harvest, to a purer sphere ;
Its calm may *we* know while, kept back, belated,
    We linger here!

Then wipe away all idle tears of sorrow ;
　　The inner sight they shall no more bedim ;
It lifts our eyes to the Eternal Morrow
　　　　To think of him !

From the fine tribute of the Rev. Dr. Frederic H.
Hedge, read at the burial, the following is taken : —

"His image is before me as he appeared in his collegiate
days, a blooming youth of abounding promise, one of the
first, if not the very first, in a class which gave to the Church
such distinguished preachers as Bellows and Osgood and
Simmons.

"How little that image changed in maturer years, and
even in this last decade of his life! Growth in knowledge,
in wisdom and experience, might deepen the expression, but
the youthful look remained. No evil passions, no jealousies
or greed or worldly ambition, wrote wrinkles in that face.
It was a face in which one might read pure thoughts, inno-
cence of soul, absence of all self-seeking and self-conceit,
meekness, humility, trust, the bosom's calm, the imper-
turbable peace of God. Age could not wither its spiritual
beauty. Years might impair his physical strength, but in
thought and feeling he could not grow old. He was one
of those to whom is vouchsafed 'the young lamb's heart
amid the full-grown flocks.'

"A man absolutely without guile, utterly unworldly, —
'a babe of Paradise' amid the scenes of this world. . . . With
what heavenly patience he bore the partial deprivation of
sight which came upon him in his later years, and with
what untiring diligence he used what remained to him of
that most precious of the senses!

"He may not rank high as a poet ; but I have never
known a more thoroughly poetic nature, never one who

had more melody in his heart. His inner life, so far as it could be interpreted by outward signs, was a daily song, a perpetual carol of gratitude and trust and hope ; and his written poetry bears that stamp of genuineness which only the poetic soul can give. . . .

" It is not my purpose, nor is this the time, to speak of the literary merits of our friend, of the arduous labors and manifold and precious service of his pen. Dearer than these to all who knew him are the beauty of his character, the charm of his converse, his childlike simplicity, sweetness, and truth. I count him one of the fairest products of our Liberal faith, and can never think of him without recalling that pregnant word which expresses the characteristic beatitude of his life, ' Blessed are the pure in heart, for they shall see God.' "

His classmate and dear friend the Rev. Samuel Longfellow wrote : —

" When I received your message, it was as if I had heard that some pure, bright raindrop had exhaled, lifted up into its native sky ; not passed out of being, but only changed in its form and become invisible to our eye. . . . What a happy, what a beautiful memory survives of a spirit and a life which, assuming nothing, pretending nothing, yet was so much ! . . .

" May I venture to say that the very name of our friend calls up such lovely visions of tranquil movement of calm waters through sunny meadows and under shady woodland coverts, such refreshment of cool waves, such rippling as of gentle laughter, or low murmured sound as of prayer ! Nothing stormy, nothing tempestuous, but calm and even flow, in gentle bounds. His very work in letters so much of it was but the reflection in the still stream of a kindred mind and heart of thoughts and fancies and feelings,

inverted in translation as the mirrored picture in the stream-
let gives back the bending grasses and the summer flowers
and the crimsoned bough of autumn."

The Rev. James Freeman Clarke testifies of
him : —

" He was always a young man to me, full of the youth
of the heart and the imagination, enjoying all things good
and fair, living as much of an ideal life as is possible to us
in a world not wholly one of poetry and beauty, but of stern
prose also and sharp trial.   Such trials he accepted, I will
not say with patience and submission, but more than that.
He took them contentedly and cheerfully, and so continued
to teach his best Christianity from the pulpit of his daily
life.

" In years he was one of the fathers of our Church, but
in temper and spirit one of its little children.   If those
who become as little children are best fitted for the king-
dom of heaven, then he who kept that divine childhood of
the heart and lived in that kingdom here must have felt
little change in going into the kingdom beyond."

The Rev. Dr. C. A. Bartol, in a communication in
the " Christian Register," said of Mr. Brooks : —

" Childhood was in him perfected into manhood by natu-
ral growth.   He was congenitally and constitutionally in-
capable of aught gross or insincere.   I have never known
a person who surpassed the impress of high honor and
magnanimity he at once and instinctively made.   A su-
perior imagination was among his gifts ; but his poetic
ardor was also a moral flame.   The red and white roses
commingled in his youthful cheeks were a true signal of
his blended candor and zeal.   His colors he never forsook.

Those whom so holy and loving a temper burns in and consumes at length are ordained prophets of another state of being, faith in which, without their character, despite reported carnal resurrections and manifestations, would decline and speedily die among men. With a joy overcoming grief, I hear the call to me to plant this tribute beside the tomb of one whose life had, beyond any flower, beauty and fragrance to my mind."

At a meeting of Mr. Brooks's late parishioners and friends in the summer of 1883 it was resolved to perpetuate his gracious memory in Newport by placing a commemorative tablet in the Channing Memorial Church. A circular setting forth this purpose was privately sent to a number of his friends and admirers at home and abroad. The response was most gratifying; young and old, rich and poor, Orthodox and Liberal, Catholic and Protestant, foreigner and native, uniting in contributing to this act of gratitude and piety. It was decided that it should take the form of a tablet and portrait medallion in bronze; and the New York artist Augustus St. Gaudens accepted the commission from the committee, which consisted of George W. Wales, John G. Weaver, William G. Weld, the Rev. Edmund B. Willson, Ann M. Smith, Mary A. Stewart, Henry C. Stevens, and the pastor. With unexpected despatch, the work was completed to the great satisfaction of the committee and the friends of Mr. Brooks in general. The memorial consists of a huge slab of black marble let into the wall on the right of the pulpit, and supported by a bevelled ledge or bracket below.

Upon this is affixed the bronze tablet, in the centre of which is the medallion, displaying in high relief a profile head and bust of Mr. Brooks, an admirable likeness and a beautiful piece of modelling. The whole work is simple and massive, yet refined in treatment. The inscription so justly sums up the personal character and services of the poet-preacher of Newport that it may be quoted as the fit conclusion to this memoir.

## In Sacred Memory

OF THE

FIRST AND BELOVED MINISTER OF THIS SOCIETY,

## CHARLES TIMOTHY BROOKS.

Born in Salem, June 20, 1813.
Died at Newport, June 14, 1883.

HIS PASTORATE EXTENDED OVER THIRTY-SEVEN YEARS.

A persuasive preacher, and eminent as a scholar and poet, he was still more distinguished for the simplicity and purity of his character, his childlike faith in God, and never-failing charity towards his fellow-men.

# POEMS.

# POEMS.

## SUNRISE ON THE SEA–COAST.

IT was the holy hour of dawn :
By hands invisible withdrawn,
The curtain of the summer night
Had vanished; and the morning light,
Fresh from its hidden day-springs, threw
Increasing glory up the blue.
O sacred balm of summer dawn,
When odors from the new-mown lawn
Blend with the breath of sky and sea,
And, like the prayers of sanctity,
Go up to Him who reigns above,
An incense-offering of love !

Alone upon a rock I stood,
Far out above the ocean-flood,
Whose vast expanse before me lay,
Now silver-white, now leaden-gray,
As o'er its face, alternate, threw
The rays and clouds their varying hue.

I felt a deep, expectant hush
Through Nature, as the increasing flush
Of the red orient seemed to tell
The approach of some great spectacle,
O'er which the birds in heaven's far height
Hung, as entranced, in mute delight.
But when the sun, in royal state,
Through his triumphant golden gate,
Came riding forth in majesty
Out of the fleckèd eastern sky,
As comes a conqueror to his tent;
And, up and down the firmament,
The captive clouds of routed night,
Their garments fringed with golden light,
Bending around the azure arch,
Lent glory to the victor's march;
And when he flung his blazing glance
Across the watery expanse, —
Methought, along that rocky coast,
The foaming waves, a crested host,
As on their snowy plumes the beams
Of sunshine fell in dazzling gleams,
Thrilled through their ranks with wild delight,
And clapped their hands to hail the sight,
And sent a mighty shout on high
Of exultation to the sky.

## THE GREAT VOICES.

A VOICE from the sea to the mountains,
  From the mountains again to the sea ;
A call from the deep to the fountains :
  O spirit ! be glad and be free !

A cry from the floods to the fountains,
  And the torrents repeat the glad song
As they leap from the breast of the mountains :
  O spirit ! be free and be strong !

The pine forests thrill with emotion
  Of praise as the spirit sweeps by ;
With the voice like the murmur of ocean
  To the soul of the listener they cry.

Oh, sing, human heart, like the fountains,
  With joy reverential and free ;
Contented and calm as the mountains,
  And deep as the woods and the sea.

## TO A YOUNG FRIEND.

How sweet to them that sail the seas
  At twilight's peaceful hour to hear,
Borne from the shore on evening's breeze,
  Familiar voices low and clear!

E'en so, as o'er the sea of time
  In life's mysterious bark we glide,
The listening spirit hears the chime
  Of memory's bells across the tide.

How sweetly fall, in summer's night,
  The moonbeams on the glimmering main!
How fair the wake of living light,
  Far-stretching o'er the mystic plain!

And memory's holy moonlight glow,
  How sweet along life's landscape shed;
Transfiguring forms of long ago,
  And summoning to life the dead!

In memory's gleam and friendship's glow,
  So may thy gliding moments shine;
And peace, as of a river's flow
  Beneath a summer moon, be thine!

And beaming down from heavens above,
  And up from memory's mirrored tide,
May stars of pure, immortal love
  Encircle thee on every side!

## ON ENTERING ST. PETER'S.

Push back the leathern curtain of the door,
And as thou standest on the marble floor,
Thou seem'st to tread on some vast, murmuring shore
Of a mysterious ocean-deep, where brood
The souls of ages, — vast infinitude ! —
Transforming to a populous solitude
The expanse of shining pavement, where the feet
Of restless crowds that pace this vast retreat
Give to thine ear an echo like the beat
Of the great surf-drum on some reboant beach ;
And the rapt fancy almost seems to reach
The music of a half-articulate speech,
Borne from some mighty continent sublime,
Peopled with shapes and thoughts of older time, —
Angels and men whose souls still Godward climb !
Thou hearest — thou rememb'rest now no more
The world without, its restless rush and roar,
Here musing on the inner, upper shore.
Sounds from the spirit's own eternal home
Float round thy soul beneath that airy dome,
Giving thy thoughts freedom to rest, and roam
On wings uplifted through the firmament,
Soaring with energies unworn, unspent,
In boundless aspiration and content.

## EVENING CHIMES OF ROME.

HEARD FROM THE PINCIAN.

THE evening sun is sinking low
    Behind Mount Mario's graceful line,
And darkly cuts the western glow
    That solitary pine.

See where, against the fading gold,
    Stands black and stark St. Peter's dome;
While in the valley, mist-enrolled,
    Twinkle the lights of Rome, —

Twinkle as when, on summer nights,
    Here, on the Campus Martius wide,
The fireflies flashed their fitful lights
    Along the Tiber's tide ;

While on the slopes and steeps around
    The moon on marble mansions beamed,
Or many a height, with temples crowned,
    In silvery starlight gleamed.

And here and there, along the hill,
    I see some lonely cypress stand,
Sombre and spectral, like a still
    Sentinel of the land, —

The holy land, where — the profane,
    Discordant present laid to sleep —
The spirit of the past again
    Its vigils soon shall keep.

But, hark! what requiem-bells are they,
    That knell o'er ages gone to rest,
As vesper-tollings chant how day
    Dies in the paling west.

To the calm land of spirits blest
    They call my restless heart to soar,
Where break thy waves, O human breast!
    And die upon the shore.

1866.

---

## PASCAGOULA.[1]

Sweet, sweet Pascagoula! so lovely and lone!
Fain would I, at parting, breathe back one faint tone
Of the witching, wild music that floats round thy
    shore,
And will float through my memory till memory's no
    more.

[1] The favorite watering-place of the Mobilians. It lies on a bay which is separated from the Gulf of Mexico by an island called Horn Island, sixteen miles long and only half a mile broad. In the summer-time a certain mysterious music is often heard there, which has been ascribed to various sources.

Fair hours! with what peace o'er my musings ye
    steal,
Too deep to confess, yet too dear to conceal!
O Nature! thy Sabbath — I spent it with thee,
In the still, solemn woods, by the silent, glad sea.
As sweet to my ear was the hymn of that morn
As if angels were singing creation just born.
And angels *were* singing, — thine angels, O Thou
To whom winds and waves chant, and the trembling
    leaves bow!
Though no human priest's accents arose on the air,
Yet the presence, O God! of thy spirit was there.
The pine with its ocean-like, spirit-like tone,
How plainly it told that I was not alone!
And was not that green, old, moss-garlanded tree
Arrayed in its robes as a priest unto Thee?
And did not a sweet choral melody rise
From woodland and waters, from shore and from
    skies?
And on the far marge of each sandy, green isle,
Did not the calm spirit of Gratitude smile?
And with her own lips did not Peace kiss the strand,
As the wave glided silently up o'er the sand?


Sweet scenes! happy hours! I must bid you farewell!
Yet aye in my memory your spirits shall dwell.
And often at eve, when the moon of young May
Beams down on my own Northern waves far away;
And often at morn, when the breeze and the light
Draw the curtain away from the dreams of the night;

And often at noon, when the birds and the bees
Hum a drowsy, sweet tune in the grass and the trees;
In the dim, solemn woods, by the silent, glad sea,
Sweet, sweet Pascagoula, I 'll still think of thee!

---

## SPRING.

Oh, tender flush of vernal dawn
    Along green fields and soft blue skies!
What sparkling of joy on the dewy lawn,
    As of myriad gleaming spirit-eyes!

The tinkle and gush of the hillside brook,
    The sunbeam's flash on the swallow's wing,
The smile that peeps from the warm, green nook, —
    'Tis the welcome of Nature to blessed Spring.

Ten thousand tongues of gladness are unsealed;
    The matin-song of brook and bee and bird,
Gay children's laugh in street and lane and field,
    And cry of bleating flock and lowing herd.

Vocal once more the budding woodland charms
    Back to his haunt the Genius of the place;
The common mother opens wide her arms
    To fold her children in her large embrace.

## CHANNING.

FROM the pure upper world to-day
　　A hallowed memory meets us here, —
A presence lighting all our way
　　With heavenly thoughts and lofty cheer.

Here first he breathed the ocean air,
　　The headland cliff exalted trod,
And felt a Spirit everywhere,
　　And saw the step of Nature's God.

His bosom, heaving with the sea,
　　Exulted in the glorious din ;
The elemental energy
　　Woke answering energy within.

In many a lone and holy hour
　　Of rapturous self-communion there,
He felt within the peace and power
　　That issue from the fount of prayer.

And in the broad blue sky above,
　　In the large book of Nature, then
He felt the greatness of God's love
　　Rebuke the narrow creeds of men.

Communing there with Nature's word,
　　Beside the vast and solemn sea,
With awe profound his spirit heard
　　The holy hymn of Liberty.

And surely here, where field and shore
  Seem waiting still his step to hear,
And, musing by the breaker's roar,
  We feel his spirit breathing near, —

Here, where the broad and chainless sea,
  The blue sky bending from above,
Confirm the gospel, large and free,
  He preached, of God's impartial love,

With an immortal fervor warm,
  Shall rise an image of the man,
That shall express the spirit's form
  As neither stone nor canvas can.

And many a soul that felt the thrill
  His look through heart and conscience sent,
Burns with the flame it kindled still,
  And is his living monument.

That flame yet lives, that life breathes power,
  The age still feels its holy thrill ;
That voice is heard in trial's hour,
  To nerve the weak and wavering will.

No time shall come when Channing's name
  Shall grow less bright on Freedom's scroll,
Or cease to light the holy flame
  Of faith and virtue in the soul.

## SIGNS OF SUMMER

### IN A COUNTRY TOWN.

SUMMER is nigh ; the balmy air is filled
With thousand omens of the blissful time.
The floating fragrances of bonfire smoke
Waft back sweet memories of life's early spring,
When from the field rose childhood's *feu-de-joie.*
At morn the robin sings his roundelay ;
The worm, unmindful of the " early bird,"
Thrusts from the new-dug earth his slimy head ;
The marshes ring with the ecstatic choirs
Of frogs exulting in the copious rain ;
The soft blue eye of May looks mildly down
With tender greeting on the face of earth,
And the bud's bosom swells responsively.
The tinkling of the cow-bell seems to chime
With the low tinkling of the rivulet,
That dances o'er the stones with silver feet.
The laugh of childhood emulates the laugh
Of gushing fountains, and a mingled hum
Of industry and pleasure, far and near,
Is borne o'er hill and valley ; soon the morn
Of spring will deepen into summer's noon.
She comes ! the blissful June ! upon the lawn
I see the sparkling of her sandalled feet ;
The sky is flushing with her rosy cheek ;
Birds, buds, and brooklets sing —
   Sweet Summer comes !

## THE DAWN OF SUMMER.

HIGH on the noiseless hill-side
   This mild May morn I stand,
And look abroad with rapture
   O'er all the enchanted land.

Below, the broad blue river
   In silent beauty flows;
Beyond, the tranquil uplands
   In majesty repose.

A hum of sweet contentment
   Is borne o'er vale and hill:
I feel the mighty heart-beat
   Through all creation thrill.

The All-Father's blue tent-curtains
   Are tenderly unfurled;
A thin blue veil hangs over
   The cradle of the world.

The earth from wintry slumber
   In grateful wonder wakes;
In myriad dreamy murmurs
   The long, deep silence breaks.

A quivering through the forest
   Stirs the expectant hush,
As prelude to the chorus
   Of praise that soon shall gush

9

From woodland and from mountain,
 From meadow, shore, and skies,
To hail the morning glory
 That greets man's wondering eyes.


The pearly gates are open;
 God's angels, flying forth,
Prepare the coming kingdom
 Of beauty on the earth.

———◆◇◆———

TO ———.

I KNOW a garden where the roses bloom
All the year round, and breathe a sweet perfume;
I know a garden where the fountains spring
All winter long, sweet music murmuring;
I know a garden where the tuneful bird
All through the seasons and the hours is heard.
Not far away o'er sea that garden lies,
In vales of Araby or Persian skies;
In every home it lies where Love presides,
In every heart it blooms where Love abides.
Love is the rose that scents that garden's bowers,
Love is the bird whose music cheers the hours;
Love is the fount that ever pulses there,
And freshens the perennial summer air; —
Love, sweet magician, clothed with HIS own might
Whose look evoked the universe from night.

*Our* home has known his spell, and knows it still;
Our hearts have known it, and forever will!
The cheek shall lose its glow, the quick pulse fail,
The fire that lit the eye grow dim and pale;
But, though all else depart, God's angel Love
Shall cheer us till we reach the home above.

MARCH 26, 1868.

---

## THE VOICE OF SUMMER.

THIS is the year's refulgent noon;
   Now, through the long midsummer hours,
The locust sings his drowsy tune,
   And roams the bee his realm of flowers.

Contentment, peace, and rapture brood —
   The smile of heaven — o'er hill and vale;
By sunny field and shady wood,
   White clouds, like wings of angels, sail.

The hills and fields, the skies and seas;
   The breath of heaven upon the brow;
Mysterious messenger, the breeze,
   That comes and goes, we know not how;

The flowers that greet us on our way,
   The carol of the summer bird;
The laugh of children at their play, —
   One gentle voice in all is heard.

## TO SAMUEL G. HOWE.

AT evening, in an Alpine vale,
    I watched the mountain-summits white
Flame rosy-red, then slowly pale
    Before the deepening shades of night.

When, from the waning face of day,
    The last faint shadow of a flush
Behind the mountains died away,
    There fell a momentary hush.

Then suddenly a thrill of awe
    Rang through the silent vale : for, lo !
That spectral mountain-chain I saw
    Lit with a preternatural glow ;

As if behind that wall of snow
    The sunken sun were shining through,
And smiling to the world below
    One more last heavenly adieu !

Who that has seen those evening shows
    Their look and voice can e'er forget ?
Can the pure world that then arose
    On the soul's vision ever set ?

Though death's pale mountains hide the sun
    Of noble lives from mortal eyes,
Oh, deem not then *their* day is' done !
    They sank, in higher heavens to rise.

As through life's twilight vale we go,
  Time's pilgrims in this earthly land,
Transpierced by that undying glow,
  How bright those shadowy mountains stand!

The boundary hills are they that rise
  And, looking on our earthly night,
Veil and reveal to mortal eyes
  The land of everlasting light.

Peace from the soul's bright track comes down
  Like evening starlight on the vale:
We see the victor's starry crown,
  And say: Farewell! farewell and Hail!

---

## THE PAST.

How oft my heart leaped up with mute delight,
When, as a boy, I journeyed home at night,
To see, while trees and lights behind us fled,
The moon and stars ride with us overhead.
So with the things of time, — like dreams they glide;
The eternal things are ever at our side.
The present moments sparkle, fade, and flee;
The Past is part of God's eternity.
Once in a tropic clime I sailed away
From a steep coast across a tranquil bay;
When, lo! behind the fast-receding shore,
Up rose the inland hills, and more and more
Lifted their greeting summits, green and clear,

And made the friendly land seem following, near.
So, as we voyage o'er the sea of time,
The Past looms up, mysterious and sublime;
Lifts its fair peaks into the tranquil sky,
And with its greeting follows as we fly, —
A spirit's welcome, with whose magic strain
Springs tender pleasure from remembered pain.
The Past is not all *passed*, not wholly dead;
Our life still echoes to its voice and tread!
The soul awakes — and, lo! like phantoms glide
The living shapes that bustle at our side:
The while our *dead* dwell on an inner mount,
Made green forever by the living fount, —
That Mount of Vision, where from Memory's mien
The veil falls off, and Hope's own eyes are seen;
While this imposing world's tumultuous roar
Dies in faint murmurs on an inland shore.

## A DARK MORNING.

Can this be morn?   I heard the cock
   Cry, long ago, the morning hour;
And through the darkness now the clock
   Speaks plainly from the neighboring tower.

And yet the mantling autumn shower,
   So cold and thick, prolongs the night;
Nor star, nor moon, nor sun hath power
   To show the faintest gleam of light.

Where'er I turn my straining sight,
  I see no living, moving form,
Save black-winged clouds in heavy flight,
  And trees that tremble in the storm.

From eastern chambers of the deep
  No day-spring breaks to greet my eyes;
But sea-born mists, wild gathering, sweep,
  Confounding earth and seas and skies.

Their endless legions rise and rise,
  The storm-wind's trumpet-blast obey, —
The scattered crown of Autumn flies
  Before that murky, grim array.

Where is the world that, yesterday,
  With tranquil beauty tranced my sight,
As, bosomed in the skies, it lay
  A paradise of love and light?

Where are the skies that met my gaze,
  And seemed to kiss the earth's fair face,
While over it the summer haze
  Hung health and beauty, glow and grace?

Wait a few hours, and thou shalt know,
  And see " with unbeclouded eye,"
Though night and grief dwell here below,
  Sunshine and gladness reign on high.

Then shall these storms of earth, that seem
    To swallow heaven, have passed away,
Like shadows of a troubled dream,
    When morning mists are lost in day.

———◆◇◆———

## THE FAITHFUL MONK.

GOLDEN gleams of noonday fell
On the pavement of the cell,
And the monk still lingered there
In the ecstasy of prayer;
Fuller floods of glory streamed
Through the window, and it seemed
Like an answering glow of love
From the countenance above.

On the silence of the cell
Break the faint tones of a bell.
'T is the hour when at the gate
Crowds of poor and hungry wait,
Wan and wistful, to be fed
With the friar of mercy's bread.

Hark! that chime of heaven's far bells!
On the monk's rapt ear it swells.
No! fond, flattering dream, away!
Mercy calls; no longer stay!

Whom thou yearnest here to find
In the musings of thy mind, —
God and Jesus, lo! they wait
Knocking at thy convent gate.

From his knees the monk arose.
With full heart and hand he goes;
At his gate the poor relieves,
Gives a blessing, and receives;
To his cell returned, and there
Found the angel of his prayer,
Who, with radiant features, said,
"Hadst thou stayed, I must have fled."

## OUR ISLAND HOME.

THOUGH here no towering mountain-steep
    Leaps, forest-crowned, to meet the sky;
Nor prairie, with majestic sweep,
    Enchants the gazer's roaming eye, —

Yet ocean's glittering garden-bed,
    Summer and winter, cheers the sight:
Its rose, the sun, at noon flames red;
    The moon, its lily, blooms by night.

The white-winged ships, in fleet career,
    Like sea-birds o'er the ocean skim;
They rise, glide on, and disappear
    Behind the horizon's shadowy rim.

So sail the fleets of clouds; and so
   Stars rise, and climb the heavens, and set,
Like human thoughts, that come and go —
   Whence — whither — no man knoweth yet.

Far onward sweeps the billowy main;
   To meet it bends th' o'erarching sky:
Of God's vast being emblems twain;
   Deep unto deep gives glad reply.

These open, each, a broad highway;
   To endless realms the soul invite:
The trackless ocean-floor by day,
   The star-lit stairs of heaven by night.

Oh, enviable lot! to dwell
   Surrounded by the great-voiced sea,
Whose waves intone, with trumpet-swell,
   The hymn of Law and Liberty!

## THE VOICE OF THE PINE.

O TALL old pine! old gloomy pine!
Old grim, gigantic, gloomy pine!
What is there in that voice of thine
That thrills so deep this heart of mine?

Is it that in thy mournful sigh
Old years and voices long gone by,
And feelings that can never die,
Come thronging back on memory ?

Is it that in thy solemn roar
My listening spirit hears once more
The trumpet-music of the host
Of billows round my native coast ?

Or is it that I catch a sound
Of that more vast and dread profound, —
The soul's unfathomable sea,
The ocean of eternity ?

## HOPE AND MEMORY.

HOPE — Memory, — blessed pair! how sweetly gleams
O'er life the lustre of their mingling beams!
There comes, e'en here on earth, full many an hour
When, by the stress of thought's transfiguring power,
Some joy or sorrow, with absorbing sway,
Swells to an age the limits of a day :
And, lo ! the sun stands still o'er Gibeon,
While softly from the vale of Ajalon
The lingering moon looks forth, and moon and sun,
Like rose and lily, weave their lights in one :
Moonrise and sunset, Hope and Memory, blend
To make the Heavenly day that knows no end !

## A LAST FLYING GLANCE AT MOUNT WASHINGTON.

OH, lovely, soul-entrancing sight!
Mount Washington's majestic height
Soared to the sky, all glistening white!

Leftward the mountain chain below
Stood stark and black against the glow
Of that high slope of dazzling snow.

In front, for miles on miles outspread,
The vale was one great garden-bed
Of crimson, gold, and flaming red.

Winter stood facing Summer there,
And through the amber autumn air
Looked forth their mutual greeting fair.

Ah! all too swiftly from my sight
Was snatched that vision of delight,
Perchance for mortal eye too bright.

But pictured on the inner eye,
These revelations from on high
Shall last when earthly shadows fly.

Beyond the reach of human art,
Engraved forever on the heart,
Such glories never can depart.

OCT. 8, 1880.

## CHARLOTTE CUSHMAN.

*( Lines suggested by her request, just before she died, to have Lowell's " Columbus " read to her.)*

For wast not thou, too, going forth alone
  To seek new land across an untried sea ?
New land, — yet to thy soul not all unknown,
  Nor yet far off, was that blest shore to thee.

For thou hadst felt the mighty mystery
  That on man's heart and life doth ever rest, —
A shadow of that glorious world to be,
  Where love's pure hope is with fruition blest.

Thine was a conflict none else knew but God,
  Who gave thee, to endure it, strength divine.
Alone with Him, the wine-press thou hast trod,
  And death, His angel, seals the victory thine.

The narrow sea of death thou now hast passed ;
  The mist is lifted from the unseen land ;
The voyage ends ; the shining throng at last
  Meet thee with welcome on the heavenly strand.

## A RHYMED HOMILY.

In the wintry twilight and firelight I sat in my
 chamber, and there
Musing I watched through the casement, in the still
 December air,
"As a cloud, and as doves to the windows," the
 white-winged feathery snow,
Like a spectral apparition, glide downward soft and
 slow.
The flakes fell pure and noiseless all over the bare
 brown land,
A downy mantle weaving, by God's mysterious hand,
The naked earth to cover, and tenderly to keep
The limbs of the weary mother through her long
 winter sleep.
So Heaven, I thought, lets gently the mantle of
 mercy fall,
And drops the veil of oblivion on the sins and sor-
 rows of all;
And the white-winged angel of pity comes down
 through the wintry gloom
Of a world unbelief hath blighted, and whispers of
 spring-time's bloom.
And I thought how this tranquil snow-fall, as a white
 cloth, would cover the bier
Where soon should lie stark and rigid the dead and
 discrownèd year,

And how graciously alighted the flakes on Memory's
    graves,
Where rested the dead in their haven from life's
    tumultuous waves.
And I read in the snow-flakes an emblem how man's
    generations flee,
And sink and melt in the ocean of cold mortality.
And the sad-eyed angel of Memory moistened with
    a tear
The cheek of Hope, her sister, as they waited the
    coming year.

.    .    .    .    .    .    .    .

I sat in the wintry twilight and mused by the chim-
    ney's glow,
And watched the sparks fly upward, as downward
    fluttered the snow.
Fitfully darted upward these "sons of the burning
    coals," —
Flew up and vanished in darkness, like hopes of
    human souls.
As I sat gazing and musing, the crackling fire
    burned on,
And another flame within me on the world of the
    spirit shone.
" Yes, man is born to trouble, as the sparks fly
    upward," I said;
" So short-lived, restless, and fitful, how quickly his
    years are fled!
But is this, then, the whole of the story the spark-
    swarms tell in their flight,
Ere their brief and bright trail upward is quenched
    in the smoky night?

Yes, man is born to trouble; but the sparks that
    *upward* fly
Give sign in their upward motion of man's true
    home on high.
The shred of flesh may wither, and melt like snow in
    the sea;
But the spark of the soul, ascending, inherits
    eternity.
Life's trials and tribulations — not out of the dust
    they come;
The troubles that man is born to are angels to
    point him home.
They come from the faithful Father, to teach man the
    upward road
That leads, though steep and rugged, to Heaven's
    serene abode."
And thus, in my fireside musings, now sate with
    me angels three, —
The angels of Hope and Remembrance and Im-
    mortality.

## THE NEW YEAR.

RELENTLESS Time, dear friends, has breathed again
Her wintry mood on Nature and on men.
Long since the recreant sun's declining power
Has clipped the merry daylight hour by hour.
Long since the feathered tribes on tireless wing
Have sought the regions of perpetual spring.
Now bound in amber chains the woodland lake

And laughing streamlet hushed to silence lie.
Now earthward softly floats the glittering flake,
   And gathering storm-clouds drift across the sky.
Dead in the hollows lie the autumn leaves,
   And through the naked tree-tops softly stirs
The spirit of the dying Year, and grieves
   In slow, sad moaning to the universe.

We stand, indeed, 'twixt two eternities
   Of Time; and one has vanished like the dew.
   Deep in its breast the stellar systems grew,
And in its dead arms now the last sun lies.
A million ages drop from life and mind
   As yesterday, when they are past, and all
   The planets circle at their central call,
And never note the years they leave behind.
The slow earth cracked and shrank 'mid rains of
      fire,
   Till through the dull mephitic atmosphere
   Young Life arose and whispered, " I am here ! "
And thrilled the universe with new desire.
Lo ! to the rhythmic chant of Time and Space
   An answering murmur chimed from budding trees,
   A rushing chorus that shall never cease
Till God hath numbered all the human race.
Far in the sand a sculptured stone appears;
   Deep on the halls of kings has grown the mould.
   Oh, Love is ever young and ever old,
And hand in hand with Time walk hates and fears.
Deep in the wondrous strata of the earth
   Bones of successive ages crystallized;
            10

Humanity lies only half disguised.
A chipped flint tells us of a nation's birth;
From out the mother liquor of events
    Precipitates the dim historic tale.
    And thou, Old Year, hast passed within the vale,
And night shuts o'er thee with her spangled tents.

Yet in this shifting, ever-present Now
    Alone is found reality of joy.
Each soul with healthy life it doth endow,
    And in its magic romps each girl and boy.
We feel the tingling of our pulse, and know
A thousand years will melt away like snow.
As some great continental artery
    Empties its flood upon the coming tide,
    And in that grand collision far and wide,
Tiptoed to heaven stands up the frothing sea:
So shall the struggle of the nations be;
    When flood-gates burst by press of passion high,
    The earth's wild wail shall plash against the sky.

---

## TO AMES'S PICTURE OF THE HAY-MAKER.

SWEET maiden, with the twofold glow
    Of health and summer on thy cheek,
Thy thoughts, thy home, I fain would know:
    Wilt thou not lift thine eyes and speak?

Alone I see thee standing there,
  The flush of toil upon thy face,
Out in the silent summer air,
  In Nature's calm, unconscious grace.

" Thy thoughts " ?   Thou art thyself a thought
  Bodied in light, — a magic form
By memory, love, and fancy wrought,
  With beauty's blissful breathings warm.

" Thy home " ?   Not here its place is found,
  Amidst the fairest fields of earth :
A purer air than ours breathes round
  The realm serene that gave thee birth.

## TO THE MEMORY OF H. N. S.

THIS is not all, — this fleeting world we see:
A fairer, purer, brighter, there must be,
Where dwell all glad and radiant souls like thee !

Where Death's eclipse no more shall cast its gloom,
Nor fell disease life's wasting lamp consume ;
Where Love's fair flowers wear amaranthine bloom ;

Where stormy wind and tempest rage no more ;
Drear Winter's long suspense forever o'er —
Peace reigns, unruffled, on that summer shore.

There, with our loved and lost, the pure and brave,
Dear Brother! thou, where palms immortal wave,
Hast found a home beyond the shadowy grave!

The soul that through thy gentle eyes beamed clear
No more in earthly light shall greet us here:
It looks upon us from a brighter sphere.

And yet we cannot feel that thou art far,
Though now thy spirit, like a tranquil star,
Beckons to where the pure and gentle are.

Farewell! God's peace we feel, sweet soul! is thine:
We would not faint, nor murmur, nor repine,
Sharing with thee, by faith, thy home divine!

MAY, 1876.

---

## LINES

COMPOSED AT THE OLD TEMPLES OF MARALIPOOR.[1]

SPEAK out your secret, bellowing waves,
    That thunder round this temple's door,
And when the lashing tempest raves,
    Leap in, and wash the sand-heaped floor!

[1] They stand on the very verge of the sea, about thirty-six miles south of Madras, where Southey, in his " Curse of Kehama," lays the scene of the chapter called " The City of Baly."

What hide ye ın your watery tomb ?
  What treasures snatched ye from the shore,
Ye sullen, restless waves that boom
  And thunder round this temple's door ?


Say, is it true, as legends tell,
  That, ages since, great Bali's town,
O'erwhelmed by your encroaching swell,
  With tower and temple, all went down ?


Speak out, thou stern old sentinel,
  That lingerest on the outer rock,
That brav'st the undermining swell,
  Defiest the overwhelming shock !


Lies there a city at thy feet,
  Far down beneath the moaning tide ?
Say (for thou know'st), the tale repeat :
  What secret do these waters hide ?


Ye all are voiceless, — silent stone,
  And sounding sea : no word ye speak, —
Nor sculptured shape nor billow's moan
  Can give the answer that I seek.


Old Ocean rolls as first he rolled
  Majestic on creation's day ;
And still their course the waters hold,
  While man and all his works decay.

Yon grim old shapes — not one of all
　Wears terror on his stony brow:
Dead sculptures line that rock-hewn wall,
　The four-armed god is harmless now.

Yet can I, as I gaze, revere
　The faith that thus, though dimly, bore
Its witness to the power that here
　Rolls in the billows on the shore.

And this, too, is the self-same sea
　That wets my native coast with spray;
And like a child it welcomes me,
　As round my feet its waters play.

Oh! could I here to idols turn,
　No human pile should be my shrine;
But, Ocean! how my heart would yearn
　To come and be a child of thine!

---

## GRANDMOTHER'S STORY.

ON HEARING IT PLAYED BY FRAULEIN LIEBE.

GRANDMOTHER sat in her old arm-chair;
The firelight gleamed on her silvery hair,

That flowed like silk from her snowy cap:
Her knitting and spectacles lay in her lap.

The grandchildren clustered on either side.
" Dear grandma, tell us a tale," they cried.

And so grandmother began and told
A wonderful tale of the days of old.

Grandmother's voice was fine and thin,
Like the far-off tone of a violin.

But was it a tale, or was it a tune,
I overheard the old grandma croon,

As I stood at the window listening there
To the tones that stole on the evening air ?

It seemed an old story I oft had heard,
Though I vainly sought to catch one word.

'T was childhood's music I seemed to hear,
Coming back to my spell-bound ear ;

A tone commingling, sweet and low,
All the dear voices of years ago :

Of mother and sister — the tender refrain
Of Mother Nature's soothing strain ;

The music of childhood's morning air,
The murmur of birds and bees was there ;

The musical patter on roof and pane
In summer nights of the gentle rain,

The patter of happy children's feet,
The ring of their voices in house and street:

All this came back to my soul with a thrill
Of rapture that haunts my memory still, —

A rapture no words can ever tell:
It steals on the heart in the plaintive swell,

The wild, the tender, human tone,
Of the whispering violin alone.

---

## ON THE DEATH OF A YOUNG ARTIST.

THE breath of morn and May,
Soft as a spirit's influence, drew him forth
    To spend with Nature one more tranquil day,
And look his last on this majestic earth.

    Reclining on her breast,
He reads once more her sweet, benignant face,
    Then peacefully to rest
Sinks like a child, there, in her great embrace.

    Alone! no human eye
Hung o'er him, as he lay, with yearning love;
    Yet God's blue, tender sky
Looked down upon him through the pines above.

So near — and yet alone !
No kindred hand to smooth his dying bed ;
    But a low plaintive moan,
As of a spirit, stirred the boughs o'erhead.


It was God's spirit near!
" For so He giveth his beloved sleep,"
    And strews the leafy bier,
And bids his angels watch around him keep.


He was — and is — at home ;
Gone hence, attended by a spirit-band,
    Where death no more can come,
He dwells now in his native spirit-land.


Was it not meet that so —
By heaven's mysterious whisper called away —
    That gentle one should go
Hence, in the tenderness of life's pure May ;


As the breeze dies away —
Mysteriously dies ;
    As dies the fading light, at close of day,
In summer skies !

## THE OLD HOMES.

THE *heart's old homes!* how many we have known!
But three, most dear of all, I call my own.
Three homes are mine: to each my spirit clings;
To each my song a grateful tribute brings.
The first, my place of birth: the dear old town
Where to my infant eyes Heaven first came down;
Where my first foretaste of its perfect bliss
Came in a mother's smile, a mother's kiss;
Where Nature's wondrous face my musings blessed;
Where Heaven upon the treetops seemed to rest.
Then that fair island, scarce less dear to me,
Embosomed in New England's *Zuyder Zee*,[1] —
The home of my adoption; where I found
Amidst the sea of life an anchoring ground;
Where the transplanted tree put forth young shoots,
And drank new life through all its clinging roots:
But yet a third sweet home I still would name,
Whose charms with equal right that title claim
Where first the Muses won my youthful love,
And drew my steps to their enchanted grove;
Where first I felt the awful, rapturous thrill
That stirs the heart beneath their sacred hill;
Drank inspiration from Castalia's fount,
And breathed the air that floats o'er Delphi's mount;
Where first I heard old Homer's trumpet clang,
And Virgil's Mantuan pipe melodious sang.

[1] Literally, South Sea.

## HARVARD'S ELM-TREES.

Aʜ! whither, when they vanished, flew
Those four fair years we journeyed through,
From '28 to '32,
    Beneath old Harvard's elm-trees ?

From '28 to '32
How sweetly beamed the noonday blue ;
How sweetly summer moons looked through
    Old Harvard's ancient elm-trees !

From '28 to '32
A band of brothers, fond and true,
What thrills of hope and joy we knew
    Under old Harvard's elm-trees !

From '28 to '32
Morn gleamed upon Castalian dew,
As, merry college birds, we flew
    Beneath old Harvard's elm-trees !

And when the glow of evening threw
Around the scene each magic hue,
How sweet the twilight rendezvous
    Beneath old Harvard's elm-trees !

From '28 to '32,
Ah! hopes were high and fears were few,
As boyhood into manhood grew
    Beneath old Harvard's elm-trees !

Then soft life's picture fancy drew,
And called our spell-bound eyes to view,
Through her enchanted avenue,
   From under Harvard's elm-trees!


Ere yet the sober truth we knew;
Or envious fate the signal blew,
That sent a wintry shiver through
   The leaves of Harvard's elm-trees.


And each live stem a mast-head grew,
Whence all the pennons seaward flew,
That summoned us to bid adieu
   To Harvard's dear old elm-trees.


Ah! moments, months, too fast ye flew
From '28 to '32;
Yet still our hearts past hours renew
   Beneath old Harvard's elm-trees.


Shades of the dead! once more with you
We live departed moments through,
And heavenly words we listen to
   Beneath old Harvard's elm-trees!


Oh! when I sink, as all must do,
Above me plant no funeral yew:
Down on my rest let stars look through
   Fair Harvard's dear old elm-trees!

Companions dear of '32,
When God in mercy leads us through
The shining gates — to me and you —
Were heaven quite heaven without the view
   Of Harvard's dear old elm-trees ?

———◆◆◆———

## THE PROPHECY OF YOUTH.

WHEN, in the pilgrimage of life, —
Its morning dreams, its midday turmoil past, —
   Led by the gentle hand of Time,
      We come at last,
   With no unwilling step, to climb
   The sunset-mountain's brow ;
Far from the din and dust of earth's bewildering
      strife,
   And, rapt in musing wonder, now
   Amidst the sober glories stand
   Of memory's autumnal land,
      And rest our toil-worn feet
From the long march ; and for the noonday's heat
Bathe in cool splendors of the evening sky ; —
      Then, as the clearer eye,
      Purged from ambition's fire
And fever-heat of passionate desire,
      Looks back, with wistful gaze,
To the fair hours and haunts of youthful days, —
      How near, indeed, how near,
In that serene and tranquil atmosphere,
Those far-off morning fields of unsoiled life appear !

Nay, 'tis not all a dream!
The fair illusion veils a fairer truth!
　　The visionary gleam,
　　The roseate glow that lie
　　Before fond Memory's eye,
On the dew-spangled landscape of our youth,
Come from a land within, that prophesies
　　A morning yet to rise
Upon the soul in these immortal skies,
That glow where Hope and Memory, hand in hand,
Hail their celestial home, their common fatherland.

　　True! in the morning of our days,
　　Hope's rainbow in the west appears,
　　And evening's backward glancing rays,
　　Shining perchance through Sorrow's tears,
　　Light up its image in the east;
　　But still, as on the past we gaze,
　　The memory of a hope, at least,
　　Life's evening hour consoles and cheers.

Yea, the remembered dreams of long ago,
As angels, cheer us on with hope's warm glow;
The morning visions fair, that hovered round
Our wayward steps on youth's enchanted ground,
Come back again, and stand revealed anew
In clearer light to manhood's calmer view.

O mystery of our being!　Endless praise
To Him who links in one our fleeting days!
Whose spirit bids, in mystic union sweet,
Boyhood and manhood, age and childhood, meet.

Then, brothers, gladly own, forevermore,
We are but children on the murmuring shore
Of that vast, mystic deep, whence saint and sage
Have caught inspiring airs in every age, —
Being's immense, unfathomable sea ;
Whose waters whisper of eternity, —
Whence never wing or line of human thought
Tidings of bottom or of bound have brought ; —
Ethereal ocean, on whose boundless breast
All worlds and souls forever ride and rest.

## A PLEA FOR FLOOD IRESON.[1]

Who is the greybeard, haggard and hoar,
Splitting to pieces beside his door
A boat hauled up on the rocky shore ?

[1] Very familiar to my childhood was the "Chant of Flood
Ireson," and thus it ran : —

> "Old Flood Oirson, for his hord hort,
> Was tor'd and futher'd and corried in a cort.
> Old Flood Oirson, for his bad behavior,
> Was tor'd and futher'd and corried into Salem.
> Old Flood Oirson, for leaving a wrack,
> Was torred and futher'd all over his back."

The people of Marblehead have been for years entirely satis-
fied that Ireson suffered unjustly, and very indignant that their
ancestors and ancestresses should be eulogized in the glowing
strains of poesy for what was only the momentary ebullition
of the rage of a parcel of wharf boys.  John W. Chadwick, a
native of Marblehead, in his charming paper on the old town

'T is old Flood Ireson — pale and spare
Are his sunken cheeks, and his fluttering hair
Is white, and wasted with age and care.

What a serpent-like sting hath a thoughtless tongue!
For fifty years the children had sung
A false and taunting song, that wrung

The old man's heart with a life-long pain,
With the memory of that wild refrain
Burning into his very brain;

Till now in the street, with bated breath,
Neighbor to neighbor whispereth:
"The poor old man is cowed to death."

Old Flood Ireson! all too long
Have jeer and gibe and ribald song
Done thy memory cruel wrong.

Old Flood Ireson, bending low
Under the weight of years and woe,
Crept to his refuge long ago.

in the July number of "Harper's Magazine" for 1874, says:
"It was in the night that the wreck was discovered. In the
darkness and the heavy sea, it was impossible to give assistance.
When the skipper went below he ordered the watch to lie by
the wreck till *dorning;* but the watch wilfully disobeyed, and
afterward, to shield themselves, laid all the blame upon the
skipper. I asked one of the skipper's contemporaries what
the effect was on the skipper. '*Cowed him to death,*' said he."

Old Flood Ireson! gone is the throng
Who in the dory dragged him along,
Hooting and tooting with ribald song.

Gone is the pack, and gone the prey;
Yet old Flood Ireson's ghost to-day
Is hunted still down Time's highway.

Old wife Fame, with a fish-horn's blare
Hooting and tooting the same old air,
Drags him along the old thoroughfare.

Mocked evermore with the old refrain
Skilfully wrought to a tuneful strain,
Jingling and jolting he comes again

Over that road of old renown, —
Fair broad avenue, leading down
Through South Fields to Salem town;

Scourged and stung by the Muses' thong
Mounted high on the ear of song, —
Sight that cries, O Lord! how long!

Shall Heaven look on and not take part
With the poor old man and his fluttering heart, —
Tarred and feathered and carried in a cart?

Old Flood Ireson, now when Fame
Wipes away, with tears of shame,
Stains from many an injured name,

11

Shall not, again in the tuneful line,
Beams of Truth and of Mercy shine
Bright through the clouds that darken thine?

---

## A PHILOLOGICAL DITTY.

YE wise ones who tell us, with infinite pains,
    What everything borrows its name from,
Once more will ye ransack your books and your brains
    And tell us where *Woman's* name came from?

We bid you not tell, for we know it full well,
    That *Man* is the finish of *Human;*
But humbly we pray, good gentlemen, say
    Why man's better half is called *Woman?*

We know too, full well, that Adam once fell,
    As the record, so ancient, doth show, man,
And that Eve was the cause of his breaking the laws;
    But must she for that be a *Woe-man?*

And this we know too, if History's true,
    If Homer once sang like a true man;
When woman draws nigh, there's that in her eye
    Which seems to say audibly: *Woo-man.*

Come, then, help us out from this thorn-hedge of doubt,
    Some kindly philosopher; do, man!
For if we should die, we cannot tell why
    The partner of *man* is called *Woman.*

## SALEM.

WHEN an old son of Salem, after years
Of exile, in his native streets appears,
Behold, in his perplexed and eager glance,
What crowds of questions yearn for utterance!
Pray, can you tell me, friend, if hereabout
There lives a person by the name of Strout?
What has become of that queer winking man,
Called "Jaquish," who *could saw a load of tan?*
Does the old green Gibraltar-cart still stop,
Up in Old Paved Street, at Aunt Hannah's shop?
Beside Cold Spring drop the sweet acorns still?
Do boys dig flagroot now beneath Legge's Hill?
When 'Lection-day brings round its rapturous joys,
Does Dr. Lang sell liquorice to the boys?
Is there a house still standing where they make
The regular old-fashioned 'Lection-cake?
Does "A True Grocer" his own merits praise?
Does Mister Joseph bake cold loaves some days?
Deputy Dutch and dog — do they still chase
The recreant debtor to his hiding-place?
Do children sometimes see with terror, still,
The midnight blaze of wood-wax on Witch Hill?
Or hail, far twinkling through the shades of night,
The cheering beam of Baker's Island Light?
Where is the old North Church that heard the tread
Of Sabbath-breaking troops from Marblehead?
Where — in what realm — do still these eyes behold,

As once, with childish gaze, in years of old,
They looked upon that holy, homely place,
The old square pews and each familiar face ?
Where the old sounding-board, that hung mid-air,
A sword of Damocles, by a wooden hair ?
Each urchin watched, with mingled hope and dread,
To see it fall plump on the parson's head.
And that dark hole beneath the pulpit stairs,
That still almost, at times, my memory scares.
What if the "tidy-man," bad boy ! should hale
Thy trembling body to that gloomy jail !
Where the knob-headed pole — the magic wand —
The dreaded ensign of his stern command ?
Full many an urchin of the gallery crew
Feared that long sceptre — aye ! and felt it too.
Little old man, thy image leads a train
Of funny recollections through the brain.
It marks a time when doubts began to grow,
If bodily shivers fanned the spirit's glow ;
When filial feet, that could not touch the floor,
Dangled and kicked till the long hour was o'er,
The last prayer closed, and seats slammed down again
With what queer Hood might call a *wooden Amen.*
Gaunt organ-blower ! how thy Sunday face
Threw o'er thee such a sanctimonious grace,
That strangers had been sometimes known to err,
And take the blower for the minister.
How in the pauses of his holy toil,
As if anointed with invisible oil,
He looked from out his cell complacent round,
Rapt with the memory of the solemn sound,

With large, contented eyes that seemed to say, —
"Have we not done the music well to-day?"

But still fresh questions crowd upon his mind,
And still sad answers he is doomed to find.
Yet while the pilgrim, roaming up and down
The streets and alleys of his native town,
So many a well-known object seeks in vain,
The sky, the sea, the rock-ribbed hills remain.
In the low murmur of the quivering breeze
That stirs the leaves of old ancestral trees,
The same maternal voice he still can hear
That breathed of old in childhood's dreaming ear;
The same maternal smile is in the sky
Whose tender greeting blessed his infant eye.
Though much has changed, and much has vanished
      quite,
The old town-pastures have not passed from sight.
Delectable mountains of his childhood! there
They stretch away into the summer air.
Still the bare rocks in golden lustres shine,
Still bloom the barberry and the columbine,
As when of old, on many a " Lecture-day,"
Through bush and swamp he took his winding way,
Toiled the long afternoon, then homeward steered,
With weary feet and visage berry-smeared.

Thus to some favorite haunt will each to-day,
At least in fond remembrance, find his way.
My thoughts, by some mysterious instinct, take
Their flight to that charmed spot we called The Neck;

Aye! round the Mother's neck I fondly cling;
Around her neck, like beads, my rhymes I string.
She will not scorn my offering, though it be
Like beads of flying foam, flung by the sea
Across the rocks, to gleam a moment there,
Then break and vanish in the summer air.


Then hail once more The Neck — the dear, old Neck!
What throngs of bright and peaceful memories wake
At that compendious name! what rapturous joy
Kindles the heart of an old Salem boy!
Within its gate a realm of shadows lay, —
A land of mystery stretching far away.
There with the ghostly past I talked, — with awe
The ancient Mother's august form I saw.
Oft in the Sabbath evening's quiet ray,
Down this old storied street we took our way
To where, beside the fresh, cool, spray-wet shore,
Old Colonel Hathorne's hospitable door
Invited us to rest; serenely there
The patriarch greeted us with musing air.
What but a bit of Eden could it be, —
That little garden close upon the sea?
Within red rose, and redder currants glow, —
Without, the white-lipped ocean whispers low.


I climb yon hill, and see, forevermore,
A spectral sail approach the wooded shore.
On Winter Island wharf I see them land,
A ghostly train comes forth upon the strand:

Reverent and brave, inflexible, sedate,
Founders and fathers of the Church and State.
A village springs to life, — a busy port;
It has its bustling wharves, its bristling fort.
Lo! Fish Street — destined one day to run down
To Water Street — now runs to Water-town.
Can fancy quite recall to-day the charms
Of those enchanting " Marble Harbor Farms " ?
Are the " sweet single roses " still in bloom ?
Still do the " strawberries " the air perfume ?
And from the flowers and shrubs that clothe the ground
Does a " sweet smell of gardens " breathe around ?
Well can we guess what charms the landscape wore
When first our fathers trod this silent shore;
And, sweetly locked in sheltering arms, that day,
Their shallop safe in " Summer Harbour " lay.
Such was the name they gave the spot when first
Upon their yearning eyes its beauty burst;
Till by a threefold, nay, a fourfold claim,
SALEM showed right divine to be its name.
For Salem they were taught of old to pray;
To peace — to Salem — God had led their way;
A spark of strife at Conant's breath had died —
" In Salem now — in Peace — we dwell," they cried.

Peace to my lingering song! and peace to thee,
City of Peace! of Pilgrim memory,
Sweet home and sacred shrine, old Salem town!
And add bright centuries to thy old renown!
No words could ever give fit thanks to thee
For all that thou hast given and been to me!

A child's warm blessing on thy fields and skies,
Thy rocky pastures dear to childhood's eyes,
Thy fresh blue waters and fair islands green,
Of many a youthful sport the favorite scene,
North Fields and South Fields, Castle Hill, Dark
       Lane, —
And Paradise, where Memory leads the train
Of her transfigured dead, whose relics lie
At rest where living waters murmur by, —
With thee my song shall close.  O patient friends,
'T is well that here my broken music ends!
So its last moan the shattered sea-wave makes,
When on the monumental rock it breaks.
Haply may these poor words, my stammering tongue
Upon its native air hath freely flung,
To the rude clang of Memory's wayward lyre,
In some true heart awake a smouldering fire;
And re-enkindle there the faith sublime,
That hears through all earth's din the Eternal City's
       chime.

## THE SUMMONS.

HEAVENWARD swells our fervent song:
Heavenly voices, clear and strong,
Cheer us, as we march along,
   Soldiers of the day!
Pilgrim-soldiers here below,
In the strength of God we go:

He his faithful sons will show
   All the shining way.

Sons of freemen! will ye be
Sons of Freedom, truly free
In the spirit's liberty?
   Each base lure tread down!
Onward, upward — daily, press!
Freedom's price is watchfulness:
This the Lord of Heaven shall bless
   And with triumph crown.

Patiently your souls possess,
Temperance, patience, godliness,
These shall give you good success,
   In your heavenward way:
Then, whate'er your lot below —
Storm or sunshine, weal or woe —
Hope, like morning light, shall grow
   To the perfect day.

---

## THE LAND AND THE FLAG.

   Comrades plighted,
   Fast united,
Firm, to death, for freedom stand!
See your country torn and bleeding!
Hear a mother's solemn pleading!
   Rescue Freedom's promised land!

In her keeping
Dust lies sleeping,
Kindled once with noblest fires;
Hark! e'en now their slumbers breaking,
Round her flag, indignant waking,
Muster our immortal sires!

Ensign glorious,
Float victorious!
Treason's gloomy hordes dispel!
Cheer the freeman sinking — dying —
Send the pallid foeman flying,
Triumph o'er the might of hell!

Night may shroud us,
Death becloud us,
Through all glooms thy stars shall shine!
Motherland, before thine altar,
Swear we ne'er to faint or falter,
Conquering — falling — still we 're thine!

1863.

## COMMEMORATION.

How beautiful the feet that slowly tread
Thy silent streets, O City of the Dead!
How beautiful the hands that bring these flowers,
The fragrant offerings of the balmy hours!
Come to the " Field of God," while flying Spring
Fans the green earth with blossom-laden wing,

And, hovering, waves farewell, ere yet she soars
Where Spring perennial gilds immortal shores, —
Come, softly lay on many an honored grave
Affection's tribute to the true and brave!


In these calm precincts of untroubled peace,
Earth's din and strife, its toil and turmoil, cease ;
And here the soldier rests from that stern strife
In which for freedom's cause he gave his life.
By day heaven's broad, blue curtain, high outspread,
The tent-roof stretches o'er his silent bed ;
And through the dusk, or soft in lunar light,
The starry flag of *Freedom* gleams by night.
How peacefully he rests ! how still and deep,
How sound and breathless his unbroken sleep !
The trumpet's call shall startle him no more ;
Nor musket's flash, nor cannon-thunder's roar,
Nor clash of steel, nor foeman's midnight tramp
Shall break the stillness of this solemn camp.


"Peace hath her victories."— Lo! God's peace is here.
From earth and sky come words of lofty cheer !
A living spirit whispers in the breeze,
A living spirit haunts the rustling trees ;
The blithe bird's carol and the floweret's bloom,
The grass-blades quivering round the silent tomb,
The teeming earth, the boundless sky o'erhead,
Proclaim : " God is the God not of the dead,
But of the living, — for to Him all live,
And to His care perpetual witness give ! "

Come, ponder here! the silence of the grave
Points to the soul where palms of victory wave.
Bring, then, your flowers, with Nature's tear-drops
    wet,
And, while the last Spring hours are lingering yet,
Lay them, with tender, reverent love, to grace
The mounds that rise above the resting-place
Where those brave souls have laid earth's armor
    down,
To wear the spirit's light and lustrous crown.

NEWPORT, May 31, 1869.

---

## DEDICATION.

UNSEEN and omnipresent Power,
    Eternal Wisdom, boundless Love,
Whose finger paints the lowliest flower,
    And strews the starry fields above!

Where shall thy glorious home be found?
    Shall man, a mote in endless space,
Lost in creation's blazing round,
    Build for his God a dwelling-place?

Lord, in our hearts thy temple build,
    Our thoughts thy chosen mansion be;
A mansion with thy spirit filled,
    Thy love, thy peace, thy purity!

# THE HOUSE OF MERCY.

HIGH up it stands, as well beseems its use.
Neighbor to Heaven that house may fitly be
Where sisters of mankind do works of Heaven.
Are they not angels, who with gentle feet
On mercy's errands tread these corridors,
And carry pleasant food and pleasant words
Of comfort, kindliness, and gentleness,
And carry twofold light to darkened rooms,
To darkened eyes and many a lowly heart?
Felicia, Benigna, Benedicta:
Happy, benign, most blessed is their work;
Happy, benign, and blessed be their names!

"Set on a hill, a city is not hid,"
Said the world's Teacher, — yet from me was hid,
While yet my eyes were strong, this gracious house;
Nor did I find it till my sight was dim,
When in that watch-tower chamber, a lone guest,
I watched and waited through the lonely night
For morn to come and bring the skilful hand
That said to the blind eye: "Let there be light."
High stands the house of mercy, as the works
Of mercy stand recorded high in Heaven.
"Whoso shall be the greatest of you all,
The same shall be your servant," saith the Lord;
And so this mansion towers above the world,
High o'er the jar and jangle of the town, —

O'er all its wranglings and its rivalries,
Lofty in place, lowly in purposes;
Glory to God and good to man its aim.
Above the world, yet in and for the world;
It seems to say, in words the heart can hear:
"They best do honor God, who most serve man."

CARNEY HOSPITAL, SOUTH BOSTON,
    Nov. 24, 1871.

## THE TRUE LIGHT.

"TRULY the light is sweet," the Preacher says.
  "Truly the light is sweet," my heart replies.
Sweet is the very memory of the days
    Whose morn and evening light once blessed my
        eyes.

Pleasant it is, and goodly, to behold
    The flower of day unfold from bud to bloom;
Or noontide bathe the world in molten gold;
    Or eve's lost fire, ere yet it sinks in gloom.

And oh! how sweet to see the stars arise,
    As, one by one, each faint and twinkling spark,
From its far home in the unfathomed skies,
    Swells the vast host that lightens all the dark.

"Truly the light is sweet," for God is light:
    Each ray a beam from his eternal eye;
And in the sweet, mysterious power of sight,
    My soul a kindred feels with worlds on high.

But sweetest is thy light, O Truth Divine!
  Thy light, O Sun of Righteousness and Grace!
That shows God's writing on this heart of mine,
  And lifts on woe's dark sea the Father's face.

## OUR POET.

THE heavens are brightening! what a shining band
  In these last days from mortal sight have gone;
  In solemn, swift procession passing on
To take their places in the Silent Land!

O white-winged fleet of souls! with joy we hail,
  As through the dusk we gaze the waters o'er,
  Gleaming beside yon calm, eternal shore,
The welcome signal of each snowy sail!

Ye, too, have reached at last the Port of Peace;
  No more on Time's tempestuous waters tossed,
  With the vast throng, before you, safely crossed,
Your anchors fall where storm and turmoil cease!

And what new stars, new constellations, glow,
  Piercing the shadows of our earthly night
  With such a strange and yet familiar light,
Making our paths more heavenly here below?

And thy pure soul has joined the noble throng
  Of our immortal ones who shine aloft
  With steadfast, starry light, serene and soft, —
Truth's champions, Beauty's heralds, Priests of Song.

Melodious minstrel! unto thee belong
  The glowing praises by the Mantuan sung
  In the sweet cadence of his tuneful tongue:
Poet Divine! (he said) to us thy song

Is grateful as the rivulet's murmuring tune
  Is to the wayworn traveller when he sips
  The gushing waters with his fevered lips,
Beneath the shade in summer's burning noon.

Such was our Poet; and where'er is heard
  The clear, strong utterance of our mother-tongue,
  Wherever English hymns or songs are sung,
His name and song are as a household word.

Who shall describe him? Can the artist's brush
  Find colors to depict the light of day,
  The breath of summer's morning to portray,
Or paint the twilight's or the midnight's hush?

His is the sunshine of the heart, the breath
  Of a pure soul by heavenly love informed,
  Of a large soul by human kindness warmed:
For such a heart, such soul, there is no death.

## AQUIDNECK.

HAIL, fair Aquidneck ! Though thine ancient name
Sound strange, Rhode Island, in the mouth of Fame,
It hath a music sweet to Fancy's ear,
To Nature, once, and Nature's children dear.
Time was when many a Narragansett heard
Melodious echoes in that homely word :
The swell and cadence of the lonely sea
Along whose marge he wandered, proud and free ;
The song the air sang where his arrow flew,
The music waves made with his light canoe ;
The sweet, though saddening moan of wind and wave,
That, haunting sandy beach and pebbly cave,
As evening fell, with low and tender sound,
Like the Great Spirit's voice, went murmuring round.

" Aquidneck " — still it speaks to Fancy's eye
Thy noble charms of sea and shore and sky :
The bold, bald rock that beetles o'er the surge ;
The bold green bank that hangs o'er ocean's verge ;
The spray-wreathed headland stretching toward the
        deep ;
The clouds that on thy far horizon sleep;
And all the beauty, majesty, and grace
Thou hast of Nature's changeful, changeless face.

Hail, pleasant isle ! how freshly shine to-day
The sky, the beach, the breaker, and the bay
Where o'er thy rocks the spray-born rainbows play !
12

Though the light deer no more thy greensward tread,
And many a song of olden days is fled,
Yet there 's a glory haunts the sapphire sky,
The emerald slope and swell — not soon shall die.
Old Ocean's bosom heaves with pride for thee;
And bends the eye of Day with love to see
Thine inland beauty and thy seaward sweep,
O fair 'midst fairest daughters of the deep!
Then hail, sweet spot! my heart's adopted home!
Where'er my feet may rest, my fancy roam;
There 's no green isle, on all the broad blue sea,
Can win away the love I bear to thee.

Aquidneck—Isle of Peace! not alway rest,
With thee, the wearied winds on Ocean's breast;
Not alway airy fingers, stretching o'er
The tuneful chords, unseen, from shore to shore,
Glide, with low tones, across the watery floor.
Yet in the maddest war of wind and wave,
By frowning cliff or hoarsely echoing cave,
Whispers transcendent Peace, her lofty form
Beauty reveals, and Grace enrobes the storm;
Till Heaven and Hope once more serenely smile
On this health-breathing, beauty-haunted isle.

O ye who here have had your childhood's home,
And ye who one brief hour of summer roam
These winding shores to breathe the bracing breeze,
And feel the freedom of the skies and seas,
Think what exalted, sainted minds once found
The sod, the sand ye tread on, holy ground!

They are gone hence, — the large and lofty souls;
And still the cliff abides, the ocean rolls;
And still, where Reason rears its beacon-rock,
The Powers of Darkness dash with angry shock.
Not here, at least, oh, let not here the soul
Yield up its thought to any low control;
Not here where, in the anthem of the deep,
And of the chainless winds that o'er it sweep,
The spirit cries with multitudinous voice:
" O man! be free, be reverent, and rejoice!"
Not here shall man, God's offspring, formed to rise
And hold communion with his native skies,
Cling to the creed that ignorance is bliss,
And indolence is glory! — not in this
Great Presence, where the vast, unresting sea
Wakes " thoughts that wander through eternity."

---

## A  REQUIEM.

THE music of the joyous bells,
    That ring to welcome Christmas in,
And echo to the song that tells
    The victory over death and sin,

Had scarcely ceased the glad acclaim,
    In memory of that blessed birth,
When Death, the dark-robed angel, came
    To call her from the woes of earth, —

Came, in the stillness of the night,
  With silent step and healing hand,
To lead her way through gloom to light,
  The glory of the heavenly land.

*He* led her home, whose lamp of love
  No wintry flood can quench or dim ;
Now, in His glorious house above,
  Her rescued spirit dwells with Him.

Send out, O bells, your gladsome voice !
  The morning breaks, the shadows flee !
Rise up, sad hearts,—rejoice ! rejoice !
  Smile through your tears,—a soul is free!

DEC. 25, 1870.

---

## A MEMORY.

As, year by year, pale autumn's leaves
  Breathe requiems by his native shore,
A spirit's voice is heard, that grieves
  For him whose form returns no more.

As, year by year, bright autumn days
  Come down from God's transparent skies,
A spirit's voice gives grateful praise
  For him whose memory never dies.

# TRANSLATIONS.

He who, with ardent, patient thought,
Through the best years of life has wrought
To shape into his mother-tongue
What best in others bards have sung, —
Has he not thus, I pray you, shown
He still loves best of all his own ?

C. T. B.

# TRANSLATIONS.

## OPENING OF THE SECOND PART OF FAUST.

*(From the German of Goethe.)*

*(A pleasant country.* FAUST, *reclining on a bed of flowers, weary, restless, and seeking sleep. Twilight. A circle of spirits, hovering in sympathy; graceful little figures.)*

### ARIEL.

*(Sings to the accompaniment of Æolian harps.)*

> WHEN the rain of blossoms falleth,
>     Fluttering, on the lap of Spring;
> When the field's green blessing calleth
>     Forth to joy each earth-born thing, —
> Great-souled elves, in stature lowly,
>     Haste to help where help they can;
> Be he guilty, be he holy,
>     Pity they the sorrowing man.

Ye, round this head in airy circles wheeling,
Come, show now, here, a noble elfin feeling:
Assuage the torment of the fevered heart;
His memory cleanse from horror's ghostly power;

Pluck out remorse's bitter, burning dart.
Four are the pauses of the nightly hour;
Haste, now, and fill them out with friendly art!
First, on the cooling cushion rest each member,
Then bathe him in the dew from Lethe drawn;
Soon will the cramped and rigid frame grow limber,
When, strong through sleep, he goes to meet the dawn.
Elves, do your fairest task to-night,
Restore him to the holy light!


### CHORUS.

*(Singly, or in bands of two or more, alternating and blending.)*

When the night-airs cool the meadows,
    Circled in with sylvan green,
Fragrant odors, tender shadows,
    Twilight conjures o'er the scene;
Lulls the heart in dreams Elysian,
    Like an infant tired of play,
On this weary mortal's vision
    Shutting-to the gates of day.

Night comes down: the landscape darkles,
    Side by side are star and star;
Greater lights and lesser sparkles
    Glitter near and gleam from far, —
Glitter here where waves are stealing,
    Gleam above in azure night;
Holy quiet's rapture sealing,
    Reigns the moon in full-orbed light.

Now extinguished are the hours,
　　Pain and bliss have fled away ;
Feel thy renovated powers !
　　Trusting, meet the new-born day !
Hills and vales in green are sleeping,
　　Bosky lids in shadow close ;
Crops, in waves of silver sweeping,
　　Fan and lull thee to repose.

Wish on wish rise crowned before thee,
　　Where yon beams of morning creep !
Light the fetters woven o'er thee,
　　Fling away the shell of sleep !
While the many loiter, dallying,
　　Boldly thou thy task fulfil ;
Clearly thinking, courage rallying,
　　Noble hearts do what they will.

(*A tremendous din announces the approach of the
Sun.*)

ARIEL.

Hark ! the Hours, in storm and thunder,
Smiting spirit-ears with wonder,
New-born Day are ushering yonder !
Rocky gates fly open clashing,
Phœbus in his car comes crashing ;
What a tumult light brings in !
Drums are beaten, trumpets sounded,
Eye is dazzled, ear astounded,
Sense confounded by the din.

Slip beneath the crowns of flowers,
Deeper nestle in the bowers,
In the rocks, behind the leaf;
If it hits you, you are deaf.


FAUST.

Life's pulses throb with fresh desire already,
Ethereal dawn with gentle welcome meeting;
Thou Earth, too, all night long, wast calm and
    steady;
And now, beneath me, thy great heart is beating.
E'en now thy choir of joys my soul surroundeth;
My spirit, kindled by thy gladsome greeting,
On toward the goal of loftiest being boundeth.
In twilight, still, the folded world lies sleeping,
With thousand-voicèd life the wood resoundeth;
Through valleys, out and in, white mists are creeping;
Yet through the depths a ray of heaven is beaming,
And twig and bough, with freshened life, seem leaping
From where they slept in gloom with odor steaming;
Húe after hue from the dark background blazes,
Where flower and leaf with tremulous pearls are
    gleaming:
A Paradise my gladdened eye amazes.


Look up! each mountain-peak its forehead hoary,
Bright herald of the solemn hour, upraises;
Thus early these may share the eternal glory,
That down to us below comes later stealing.
Each Alpine meadow, lake, and promontory

Behold it now in clearest light revealing,
And step by step it lower creeps and nigher.
He blazes forth! and ah! with blindness reeling,
I turn away, pained by the stinging fire!

Thus is it, then, when yearning long and hoping,
Up to the topmost height of fond desire,
We see fulfilment's gates their wings wide oping;
But now there burst from those eternal places
Such floods of flame, we stand there dazed and
      groping:
Life's torch we 'd light, when, lo! before our faces
A fiery sea that every sense devours —
Is 't Love, or Hate? — within whose hot embraces
Now bliss, now woe, the heart by turns o'erpowers;
So that to Earth again we look, with yearning,
To hide in youthful veil of greenest bowers.

Let then the Sun behind my back be burning!
The cataract, that through the rock-cleft crashes,
To that with growing rapture am I turning.
From crag to crag in headlong speed it dashes,
In thousand, thousand silver cascades tumbling,
And flinging high its foam in snowy flashes.
But how majestic from the roar and rumbling
Upsprings the rainbow's arch, a rosy bower,
And sprinkling round the fragrant cooling shower:
Fair image that of all man's frail endeavor;
There shalt thou well discern in thoughtful hour;
The glittering radiance pictures life forever.

## JOAN OF ARC'S FAREWELL TO HER HOME.

(*From the German of Schiller.*)

FAREWELL, ye mountains, ye beloved pastures,
And peaceful, friendly valleys; fare ye well!
Joan no more along your paths may wander;
She bids you now a fond, a last farewell:
Meadows that I have watered, trees I planted,
Long may your smiling green my kindness tell;
Farewell, ye cooling grottos, murmuring fountains,
And thou, soft Echo, voice of the lone dell,
That oft mad'st answer to my jocund strain; —
Joan may never visit you again!

Ye scenes where all my quiet joys were found,
I leave you here behind forevermore;
Ye lambkins sporting on the flowery ground,
Soon, a lost flock, ye 'll roam the mountains o'er:
I go to lead another flock, 'mid sound
Of drum and trumpet, on a field of gore.
A spirit's voice hath summoned me, — I yield;
No earth-born passion spurs me to the field.

He who of old on Horeb's height came down,
And from the burning bush to Moses spake, —
Who bade him stand and brave stern Pharaoh's
        frown, —
Who bade the shepherd-son of Jesse take

A warrior's spear and wear a kingly crown,
Who still loves shepherds for his mercy's sake, —
To me hath spoken from yon whispering tree:
" Go forth ! thou shalt on earth my witness be !

" Go, and henceforth the brazen armor prove ;
Bind the steel breastplate to thy tender breast :
Let not man's love have power thy heart to move,
Nor wild, unholy fires thy soul molest ;
No bridal wreath shall bloom thy brow above,
No smiling infant on thy bosom rest :
Yet shall the hero's lasting fame be thine ;
Above earth's noblest daughters thou shalt shine.

" When in the shock of fight the mightiest reel,
When the last hour of France is drawing nigh,
Then shalt thou wave my oriflamme on high ;
Like corn before the reaping maiden's steel,
Low in the dust shalt see the tyrant lie ;
Roll back his proud, triumphant chariot wheel,
To the brave sons of France salvation bring,
Deliver Rheims, and crown thy rightful king."

The Lord of Hosts hath promised me a sign,
And now he sends this helmet — 't is from him !
Its iron touch nerves me with power divine ;
I feel the glory of the cherubim :
I must away to join the bristling line —
A tempest whirls me onward ; earth grows dim ;
The din of battle summons me away ;
The war-steed prances, and the trumpets bray.

## A CANZONE.[1]

*(From the Italian of Dante.)*

LOVE, who, within my mind, to me discourses
About my lady, ofttimes doth inspire,
By telling things of her, such warm desire,
That then the intellect, bewildered, strays.
His gentle speaking such sweet awe enforces,
The soul that hears, and feels the tender fire,
Cries: "Leave me, for I never can aspire
To tell, as thus I hear, my lady's praise!"
And, sure, 't were meet to spare from my poor phrase,
If what I hear of her I would declare,
First, what my intellectual power transcends
And what it apprehends,
In great part, which to speak I should not dare.
But if my rhymes should not escape defect,
That venture on the praise of one so rare,
For this be blamed the feeble intellect,
And our poor speech, that has not equal worth
All that which Love says, fitly to set forth.
The sun, that circles all the world with fire,
Sees nought so fair as in that hour which shines
Above the part where she, whom in these lines

---

[1] The Canzone which forms the subject of the Third Trattato of the "Convito" of Dante, — the celebrated song which he represents himself as hearing from the lips of his old friend, the musician Casella, in the second canto of the "Purgatory."

Love makes me praise, hath her abiding-place.
All intellects, above, her charms admire:
And whoso, here below, enamoured pines,
Within his thoughts her image only finds,
When from his soul Love's peace each cloud doth
    chase.
Her being pleases so the Lord of Grace
That He his virtue still on her doth pour
In measure, past our nature's asking, free.
Her soul of purity,
Which of that health receives from Him such store,
By what she bringeth, gives of Him clear signs;
Her beauty on all visible things flows o'er,
Till e'en the eyes of those 'mid whom she shines
Summon with speed their hearts' desires to rise,
That straight take air, and issue forth in sighs.
Virtue divine from God, in her, descends,
As in the angel who sees God, to dwell;
And what fair lady doubts the thing I tell,
Let her walk with her, and her acts admire.
There, where she speaks, from Heaven an angel bends,
Who kindles in our souls the faith full well
How the high worth she has doth far excel
The uttermost whereto we dare aspire.
The gracious acts that all behold wrought by her
Go calling Love with signs no heart mistakes,
In such a voice that each can feel him stir.
It may be said of her:
Whate'er in her is found becomes her sex;
As it resembles her, is Beauty fair:
And one might say, her very aspect makes

What seemed miraculous take Nature's air.
Whence to our faith a mighty help is given;
So was she formed eternally by Heaven.
Things do appear to us in her aspect,
That bring the joys of Paradise to sight;
In her sweet smile, I say, and eyes of light,
That charm Love there, as 't were his proper seat.
They overmaster all our intellect,
As the sun's rays a fragile vision smite;
And as to gaze on her confounds me quite,
To be content with scanty speech were meet.
Her beauty rains fine flames of fire so fleet,
With such a noble spirit animate,
That all good thoughts to life, enkindled, wake,
And, as with thunder, break
The innate vices that make vile our state.
Then let each lady, self-reproached that she
Her beauty wears not lowly and sedate,
Behold this pattern of humility,
That humbleth every proud one and perverse:
I speak of Her who moves the universe.
My song, thou contradictest, to the ear,
A sister whom thou hast, it seems to me;
For this same lady, made so meek by thee,
Cold and disdainful she believes, most sure.
Thou know'st that Heaven is always bright and clear,
And in itself from all disturbance free;
But many a time our eyes are dark, and we
Then call the stars themselves, sometimes, obscure;
So when she blames for pride this lady pure,
Not as the truth doth stand, of her she deems,

But only after that which doth appear;
For I was seized with fear,
And fear so yet, that still to me she seems
Proud, when I feel her eyes do look my way.
This, if excuse thou need'st, thy judge shall hear;
And when thou canst, repair to her and say:
" Madonna, if thou not displeasèd be,
In every quarter will I speak of thee."

---

## THE WAVE.

*(From the Italian of Metastasio.)*

THE wave from the ocean dissevered,
Goes murmuring through valley and mountain:
A pilgrim it hies in the river,
A prisoner it lies in the fountain;
Sighing and moaning forever,
Till home to the ocean it flows, —
The ocean whence first it ascended,
And where, its long wanderings ended,
Its hope is at last to repose.

## A MORNING GREETING TO THE SEA.

*(From the German of Heine.)*

THALATTA! Thalatta!
Hail to thee! hail! thou infinite sea!
Hail to thee! hail! ten thousand times
My bounding heart greets thee!
As whilom ten thousand
Greek hearts leaped up to greet thee, —
Misery-vanquishing, homesick, and languishing,
World-renowned Greek hearts heroic.

The billows were swelling,
Were swelling and sounding;
The sunbeams were flashing and playing,
Refulgent with rosy lustre:
Uprose the flocks of startled sea-mews
Wheeling away, loud-screaming;
'Mid stamping of war-steeds and clattering of bucklers,
It rang through the welkin like triumph shout:
          Thalatta! Thalatta!

Welcome once more, thou infinite sea!
Like voices of home, thy murmuring waters;
Like dreams of my childhood, sunbeams and shadows
Flit o'er thy weltering billowy domain.
And memory forever renews the old story
Of all the precious, glorious playthings,

Of all the glittering Christmas presents,
Of all the branching trees of red coral,
Gold fishes, pearls and shells of beauty,
The secret stores thou treasurest up
Below in thy sparkling crystal house.

Oh, how long have I languished in dreary exile!
Like a dry, withering flower,
In the tin case of the botanist pining,
So lay my heart in my breast.
I seem like one who, the livelong winter
A patient, sat in a dark sick-chamber,
And now I suddenly leave it,
And, lo! in her dazzling effulgence,
Comes the emerald Spring, sun-wakened, to greet me,
And the rustling trees, white and blossoming, murmur,
And the fair, young flowers look up at me
With radiant, sunny glances:
All is music and mirth and beauty and bliss,
And through the blue heavens the warblers are singing,
       Thalatta! Thalatta!

Thou valiant, retreating heart!
How oft, how bitterly
Harassed thee the Northland's barbarian maidens!
Bending their great eyes upon thee,
Fiery arrows they darted;
With words all crooked and polished
Threatened to rend my bosom asunder;
With arrow-head billets they smote to destroy
My wretched, bewildered brain.

Vainly I held up my shield against them;
The arrows came hissing, the blows fell crashing,
And pressed by the Northern barbarian maidens,
Fought I my way to the sea —
And now I breathe freely once more,
And breathe out my thanks to the sea,
The blessed, the rescuing sea!
          Thalatta! Thalatta!

---

## SALUTATION OF THE SEA.

*(From the German of Count Auersperg, " Anastasius Grün.")*

BOUNDLESS, measureless, and endless,
    Type of that unknown To-be,
Bright and calm thou spread'st before me,
    Holy and eternal sea!

Shall I come with tears to greet thee,
    Tears that sorrow loves to shed
When she wanders through the graveyard
    Weeping o'er her precious dead ?

For a still and mighty graveyard,
    One vast sepulchre thou art;
Cold and pitiless thy waters
    Roll o'er many a hope and heart.

Neither cross nor gravestone whispers
   Where they sleep in calm and storm ;
Only on the shore goes weeping
   Many a monumental form.


Or shall I with rapture hail thee,
   Rapture such as thrills the soul
When the eye, a blooming garden,
   Sees its widespread charms unroll ?


For a boundless, glittering garden
   Art thou, broad and lustrous deep !
Noble blossoms, priceless treasures,
   In thy crystal bosom sleep.


Like a garden's rich enamel
   Lies thy surface smooth and green ;
Beds of pearl and groves of coral
   Are thy flowers that bloom unseen.


Like still roamers through a garden
   Ships across thy waters go ;
Seeking treasures, bringing treasures,
   Hopes and greetings, to and fro.


Tears of woe or tears of rapture,
   Which, old Ocean, shall be thine ?
Idle doubt, unmeaning question,
   Since, indeed, no choice is mine !

Since, indeed, the deepest rapture
From my eye in tears distils,
As the flush of morn and evening
Still with dew the flower-cup fills.

Tearful eyes to God I lifted
'Neath the great cathedral's dome ;
And with tears I greeted lately
My loved land, my long-sought ho

Bathed in tears, my arms I opened,
When my darling greeted me ;
On the hill I bowed me weeping,
Where I first caught sight of *thee !*

---

## O HOLY SEA!

(*From the German of Rückert.*)

O CRADLE of the rising sun, O holy Sea!
O grave of every setting sun, O holy Sea!
O thou in balmy night outspreading the crystal
mirror
Where Luna looks, a silent nun, O holy Sea!
O thou in silent midnight's chiming, through thy
wide realm,
With starry choirs, — sweet unison, — O holy Sea!
The morning's and the evening's red bloom out from
thee,

Two roses of thy garden bed, O holy Sea!
O Amphitrite's panting bosom, whose heaving waves
Now swell, now sink, beneath the moon, O holy Sea!
O Aphrodite's womb maternal! bring forth thy child,
And borrow splendor from thy son, O holy Sea!
Sprinkle the earth's green wreath of spring with
        pearly dew,
For thine the pearls are every one, O holy Sea!
The Naiads of the meadows all, that sprang from
        thee,
Come back as Nereids at thy call, O holy Sea!
The ships of thought sail over thee — and sink in thee;
Atlantis rests there, mighty one, O holy Sea!
The beaker of the Gods, that fell from high Olympus,
Hangs on the coral twigs, far down, O holy Sea!
A diver in the sea of love is Freimund's song,
Would show how rich his chosen one, O holy Sea!
My spirit yearneth like the moon to sink in thee;
Forth send me from thee like the sun, O holy Sea!

---

## A WINTER DAY.

*(From the German of Rückert.)*

Stainless beauty, winter day!
    Heaven's pure beams alone are living;
And no earth-born passion may,
    Frost-bound, sign of life be giving.

Glorious sun! a smile like this
　　Wings my soul for high aspiring;
Not a wanton's wily kiss
　　All my veins to uproar firing.

This chaste snow that sheets the expanse,
　　Hides no serpent of delusion;
In this tranquil, heaven-blue glance
　　Lurks no storm-seed of confusion.

That I, breathing summer-glow,
　　Ever lay, in bliss Elysian,
Drunk with fragrance, seemeth now
　　Like a dim remembered vision.

Ah, 't is rapture at its height
　　Thus to stand by earth unholden,
Heavenly beauty, in thy light,
　　Cold and brilliant, pure and golden!

————◦◦◦————

## SAD SPRING.

*(From the German of Rückert.　One of the Series of Sonnets
" In Memory of Agnes.")*

" Sweet Spring is here," I heard men say and sing;
Then went I forth to seek where he might be.
I found the buds on every bush and tree,

But nowhere could I find my darling, Spring.
Birds hummed; the bees, they sang: but everything
  They sang or hummed was sad as sad could be.
  Rills gushed, but all their waves were tears to me.
Suns laughed, — no joy to me their looks could bring.
Nor of my darling could I find a trace,
  Till with my pilgrim-staff I took my way
To a well-known, but long-neglected place,
  And there I found him, Spring! Near where *she*
    lay,
He sat, a beauteous boy, with tearful face,
  Like one who weeps above a mother's clay.

---

## A GHAZAL.

(*From the German of Rückert.*)

I SAW a kingly Eagle soar sunward through the air;
And in the shadow cooing, of turtle-doves a pair.
I saw the East Wind driving his cloud-flocks up the
    heavens;
And in the field a shepherd, his lambkins tending
    there.
I heard the Stars inquiring: "When, Father, shall we
    rise?"
And Germs in corn-grains groaning: "How slow the
    night-hours fare!"

I saw at morn a grass-blade bloom out, and fade ere
    night,
And storms of thousand winters the cedar's glory
    spare.
I saw the waves of Ocean, their crowns of foam cast
    down
Before the rock, like kneeling kings upon the altar-
    stair.
I saw a dew-drop sparkle, a jewel in the sun,
That dreaded not the danger of withering in the
    glare.
I saw men swarm in myriads to build their streets
    and towns;
And ants in millions rearing their hills with toil and
    care.
I saw the war-steed trampling on city and on land;
I saw his hoofs, all blood-stained, a rose-red color
    wear.
I saw, with snow-flakes, Winter weave Earth a rai-
    ment white,
When, stript of Summer's glory, she naked lay and
    bare.
I heard the shuttle whizzing to weave the sun-veil's
    gauze;
I saw a silk-worm weaving his grave of thread-like
    hair.
I saw both great and little, and saw the smallest
    great,
For I beheld God's likeness in all things everywhere.

## THE NEW BODY.

*(From the German of Rückert.)*

EARTH shall give back to me the form she held in
     trust;
No more of what was mine shall moulder in the dust.
The raiment I laid off and gave the grave to keep,
I shall put on again, when I have slept my sleep:
The same old garment still, yet new and clean and
     bright;
The mother for her child has washed it over night.

---

## AT THE DOOR.

*(From the German of Rückert.)*

I HAVE knocked at the door of Luxury;
They reached from the window a penny to me.

I have sought Love's house, and knocked at the door;
But fifteen others stood there before.

I knocked at Honor's castle gate;
"We open only to knightly state."

I visited Labor's dwelling low,
But I heard there only wailing and woe.

I asked where Contentment's house is found,
But no one knew it the country round.

But I know a house both lonely and still;
I 'll knock there at last by the Father's will.

There dwells, indeed, full many a guest,
But yet there is room for many to rest.

---

## QUATRAINS.

*(From the German of Rückert.)*

SEE, the rose-bed of creation
    Never of its flowers is bare ;
Fades one rose-cheeked generation,
    Lo ! another crop is there.

---

SPRING is a poet; wheresoe'er he looks
    Trees bloom and all the fields are gay.
Autumn 's a critic; dead leaves strew the brooks,
    Touched by his breath, and Nature's charms decay.

---

THERE 's many a little book that reads right nice,
    The reader never cares to see again ;
But whatsoe'er is not worth reading twice
    Was not worth reading once, I do maintain.

THE dog is born a slave to be;
　The will of his lord for law holds he:
But the cat is a creature born to be free;
　Thou play'st not with her, she plays with thee.

---

## THE BIRDS OF NOTRE DAME.

*(From the French of Victor Hugo.)*

'NEATH the high vaults of Notre Dame
　The nests of birds arrest my eyes;
New angels, there they sing their psalm,
　As in a nook of Paradise.
Without surprise I see them there,
　For are not they Heaven's children too?
To lodge within a house of prayer —
　What thing more natural could they do?
　　"O little birds, that sing so sweetly there,
　　Remember us in your melodious prayer!"

The holy temple is their cage,
　The heavenly water too they share;
And on the towers, of hoary age,
　They walk abroad, when skies are fair.
But when the bell sounds out for prayer,
　And the high altar's all ablaze,
They seek their cote, and, sheltered there,
　In secret gurgle forth their praise.
　　"O little birds, who sing so sweetly there,
　　Remember us in your melodious prayer!"

They sing in turn their sacred lay,
  Nor tremble at the great bell's boom,
That hails the infant born to-day,
  Or sounds the death-march to the tomb.
Their warbled praises soar on high,
  With envy seraphs list the lay;
And when a bridal train draws nigh,
  One hears the happy couple say:
    "O little birds, who sing so sweetly there,
    Remember us in your melodious prayer!"

---

## THE POST-BOY.

*(From the German of Gruppe.)*

THE stage-coach, through the forest,
  Rolls by at dead of night;
The passengers all sleeping,
  But the post-boy's eyes are bright.

Before the woodman's cottage
  What means the post-boy's blast?
The passengers are startled:
  "The station's reached at last?"

Such lovely airs his bugle
  Sends up through the window near,
It wakes the woodland echoes,
  And the moon comes out to hear.

Shine in, fair moon, at the window,
  And let my darling see
Glide through her dreams the moonsprites,
  To the post-horn's melody.

## THE KISS.

*(Spanish love-ditty from Arentsschildt's "Voices of the People.")*

SINCE my mother scolds me, dearest,
  For the kiss I gave to thee,
Give, oh, give me back, I pray thee,
  What thy lips did take from me.

Give the kiss, oh, give it freely,
  That her wrath its course may run;
So that we may tell her truly
  That the deed is now undone.

It will be for thy advantage
  If thou quickly doest this;
Give, oh, give me now, my darling,
  If thou lovest me, that kiss.

Give the kiss, for God's sake, give it!
  Mother — Heaven knows what she'll do!
Fie! I said, give back *one* only,
  And, instead, thou now hast two.

# THE PATIENT HEALED AGAINST HIS WILL.

*(From the German of Langbein.)*

A HOLY man of weight and dignity
Once passed through cities, towns, and villages;
With what intent, the Muse informs not me,
And whoso will, that reads, may guess.
Wonders his heralds were, where'er he came:
Before him leaped a throng of halt and lame;
They heard his praises sounded by the dumb,
And blind men joyed afar to see him come.

Two cripples who had hitherto
Found bread-fruit blossom on the dry old crutch,
Feared the good news were true,
And dreaded the physician's touch.
They fled from him o'er hill and dale
When he was yet three miles away;
But what could all their breathless haste avail?
By chance there came that self-same road a ray —
A health-inspiring breath upon the gale.
A viewless stroke snatched from each beggar's hand
The wood that had supported him till then;
And, in a twinkling, on their feet they stand,
A couple of restored and — ruined men.

# THE HAPPY MARRIAGE.

*(From the German.)*

ALL praise to wedlock's God be chanted!
The sight I wished for has been granted:
    I've seen one really happy pair;
Who neither grief nor discord proving,
Equally true, equally loving,
    In wedded life contented were.

Whate'er he chooses, that she chooses;
What she rejects, that he refuses:
    Two spirits guided by one will.
Untouched by selfish, earth-born trouble,
Their sorrows healed, their joys made double,
    The stream of love flows smooth and still.

As he by no set whim befooled is,
And she by no ambition ruled is,
    So neither he nor she is lord.
They ruled; but only by persuasion.
They strove; but when they did, the occasion
    Came only from their sweet accord.

As we, before the nuptial hour,
Conceal our faults with all our power,
    False each to each in foolish love;
So they, while free from all pretences,
In times of tenderest confidences,
    From all offences free did prove.

14

The last of days spent this side heaven,
The last fond kiss in this world given,
   Fresh as the first to them did seem.
They died. "When?"  Friend, thou art thick-headed!
Just eight days after they were wedded,
   Else this a fable were and dream.

———◆———

## SAINT ANTHONY'S FISH SERMON.

*(From a German versification of a passage of Abraham a Sancta
Clara, a Jesuit preacher of the seventeenth century.)*

SAINT ANTHONY one day
Found the church empty Sunday;
So he goes to the river,
A discourse to deliver.
They're ready to listen;
Their tails flap and glisten.

The carps, those old scorners,
Came out of their corners,
Their carping suspended,
Their jaws wide extended
(Ears wanting), to swallow
Remarks that might follow.

The pouts — cross-grained pouters,
Those well-known come-outers,
For this once *go-inners* —
Confessed themselves sinners.

The pouts said they never
Heard sermon so clever.

Crabs and mud-turtles, also,
That generally crawl so,
And in dirt their heads bury,
Came up in a hurry.
Crabs and turtles had never
Heard sermon so clever.

Eels and sturgeons, — best livers
Of all in the rivers, —
Forsaking their dinners,
Confessed themselves sinners.
Eels and sturgeons had never
Heard sermon so clever.

And lastly those odd fish
We mortals call codfish,
Their glass eyes distended,
Devoutly attended,
Like rational creatures,
This greatest of preachers.

And dog-fish and cat-fish,
And flounders and flatfish,
And, finally, all fish,
Both great fish and small fish,
Came swimming and squirming
In shoals to the sermon ;
And all said they never
Had heard one so clever.

When sermon was ended
To their business all wended :
The pikes to their thieving,
The eels to good living ;
The crab still goes crooked,
The codfish is stupid ;
Yet none of them ever
Heard sermon so clever.

———•◦•———

## THE PATIENT.

(*From the German of Gellert.*)

A MAN long plagued with aches in joint and limb,
Did all the neighbors recommended him,
But, for all that, could nowise gain
Deliverance from his pain.
An ancient dame, to whom he told his case,
Made up a most oracular face,
And thus announced a magic remedy :
" You must," said she,
(Mysteriously hissing in his ear,
And calling him "my dear ! ")
" Sit on a good man's grave at early light,
And, with the dew fresh-fallen over night,
Thrice bathe your hands, your knee-joints thrice ;
'T will cure you in a trice :
Remember her who gave you this advice ! "

The sick man did just as the grandam said ;
(What will not mortals do, to be
Relieved of misery ?)
Went, bright and early, to the burying-ground,
And on a grave-stone ('t was the first he found)
These words, delighted, read :
"Traveller, what man he was who sleeps below,
This monument and epitaph may show.
The wonder of his time was he,
The pattern of a genuine piety ;
And that thou all in a few words mayst learn,
Him Church and School and Town and Country
      mourn."

Here the poor cripple takes his seat,
And bathes his hands, his joints, his feet ;
But all his labor 's worse than vain,
It rather aggravates his pain.
With troubled mind he grasps his staff,
Turns from the good man's grave and creeps
On to the next, where lowly sleeps
One honored by no epitaph.
Scarce had he touched the nameless stone,
When, lo ! each racking pain had flown.
His useless staff forgotten on the ground,
He leaves this holy grave, erect and sound.

"Ah !" he exclaimed, " is there no line to tell
Who was this holy man that makes me well ? "
Just then the sexton did appear ;
Of him he asked, "Pray, who lies buried here ? "

The sexton waited long, and seemed quite shy
Of making any sort of a reply.
"Ah!" he began at length, with deep-drawn sigh,
" God's mercy on us! 't was a man,
Placed by all honest circles under ban,
Whom scarcely they allowed a decent grave,
Only a miracle whose soul might save ;
A heretic, and what is worse,
Wrote plays and verse ;
In short, to speak my full conviction,
And without fear of contradiction,
He was an innovator and a scound—"
"No!" cried the man, "no! I 'll be bound!
Not so, though all the world the lie repeat ;
But that chap there who sleeps hard by us,
Whom you and all the world call pious,
He was no doubt a scoundrel and a cheat."

---

## FATHER ADAM.

(*From the German.*)

ADAM in Paradise to sleep was laid ;
Then was there from his side a woman made.
Good Father Adam! much it grieveth me,
That thy first sleep thy last repose should be.

## A SAIL.

*(From the German.)*

OVER the shining waves dances our boat!
  O'er us the sky's blue glance,
  Round us the green expanse;
Over the shining waves dances our boat!

See how the white swan floats tranquil and free!
  See her with stately pride
  Breast the blue waves aside!
See how the white swan floats tranquil and free!

Glide we o'er life, my friends, as glides our boat!
  Glad with the sense of youth,
  Calm in the trust of truth,
Glide we o'er life, my friends, as glides our boat!

## LONGING FOR SPRING.

*(After the German of Jäger.)*

COME, lovely May, enwreathing
  Our walks with fragrant bloom,
Where violets, sweetly breathing,
  The rivers' banks perfume.
Oh, joy, once more to wander
  By vale and mountain-side,
Where flower-lined streams meander
  Through meadows far and wide!

Come, still our long, long yearning,
  The captive heart set free,
And change the children's mourning
  To joy and jubilee !
Oh, come, white lilies bringing,
  And red, red roses, too,
The nightingales all singing,
  And many a sweet cuckoo !

---

## NIGHT IN ROME.

*(From the German of Kinkel.)*

ALL streets and squares are sleeping
  In the deep hush of night ;
From the calm blue of heaven
  The pale moon pours her light.

Both lie in deathlike stillness,
  The old Rome and the new ;
And even their giant sentry,
  St. Peter's Dome, nods too.

Yet all night long the murmurs
  Of plashing fountains creep :
These keep the soul still wakeful
  That fain would sink to sleep.

Forth from the heart comes gushing
　　The old eternal song ;
In the blue moonlight's glimmer
　　The old tune sweeps along.

———◆◆———

# THE THREE GREAT CHRISTIAN FEASTS.

(*From the German of Falk.*)

　　O HEART-BRIGHTENER !
　　Sorrow-lightener !
Soul-enrapturing Christmas-tide !
　　World lay in sadness,
　　Christ's birth brought gladness ;
Joyfully, Christian heart, sing far and wide!

　　O heart-brightener,
　　Sorrow-lightener,
Soul-enrapturing Easter-tide !
　　World lay enshrouded,
　　Christ rose unclouded ;
Joyfully, Christian heart, sing far and wide!

　　O heart-brightener,
　　Sorrow-lightener,
Soul-enrapturing Whitsuntide !
　　World's inspiration,
　　Christ's new creation, —
Joyfully, Christian heart, sing far and wide!

## THE HOLY NIGHT.

*(From the German of Mohr.)*

SILENT night, holiest night!
Moonbeams form silvery light.
Hark! the tidings from star to star,
Borne by angels from near and far,
Jesus the Saviour is born!

Silent night! holiest night!
Shepherds first tell the sight!
Spread the tidings o'er hill and plain,
Bethlehem wakes to hear the strain:
Jesus the Saviour is born.

———•◦•———

## JESUS OF NAZARETH.

*(From the German of Zimmermann.)*

O THOU whose name I speak out, burning
To hear it hourly named in vain!
For whose return my soul is yearning!
How long thy field has fallow lain!

For centuries now they have contended
If thou beginning hadst or not;
Whether thou hast to heaven ascended:
Yet thee — ah! thee they have forgot.

They cling around thy cradle lowly,
   Around thy cross, thy rock-hewn bed ;
With thine own blood their hands unholy
   Paint thy fair features gloomy red.

Yet no one burns with noble fire
   To tread the pathway thou hast trod ;
None needs, forsooth, to God aspire,
   And so they worship thee as God.

It bows my heart with shame and sorrow,
   O light divine of manhood ! when
I see that they, thy name who borrow,
   Are almost everything but men.

My worship to thy life is given,
   Thou noble man in form divine !
My faith — to strive as thou hast striven ;
   To make thy work, thy being mine !

---

## THE WANDERER IN THE SAWMILL.

*(From the German of Justinus Kerner.)*

Down in the sawmill yonder
   I sate not long ago,
And heard the mill-wheel thunder,
   And watched the waves below.

I saw the white teeth gnawing;
　　I gazed as in a dream,
As they long lanes went sawing
　　Right through a pine-tree's beam.

The pine with life seemed quivering;
　　In mournful melody,
Through all its fibres shivering,
　　These words it sang to me: —

"In good time this way guided,
　　O wanderer, thou art!
For thee, for thee, hath glided
　　The sharp steel through my heart!

" For thee, when thou shalt number
　　A few days more, O guest!
This wood a place of slumber
　　Shall frame in earth's deep breast."

Four planks fell down before me:
　　No word my lips could say;
A palsying chill came o'er me,
　　The mill-wheel ceased its play.

## "AS SORROWFUL, YET ALWAYS RE-JOICING."

*(From the German.)*

LONELY ? lonely ?   No, not so, not so !
  For in spirit the true-hearted
  Round me press, from whom I parted
Years — ah ! years ago.

Joyful ? joyful ?   No, not so, not so !
  For I feel a painful yearning
  Homeward, and the tear-drops, burning,
Down my sad cheeks flow.

Gloomy ? gloomy ?   No, not so, not so !
  For I see the well-known faces,
  And I feel the fond embraces :
They are near, I know.

Hopeful ? hopeful ?   Ay, 't is so, 't is so !
  Once again to be united
  To the hearts in friendship plighted, —
With such hope I glow !

# GOOD–NIGHT!

*(From the German of Theodor Körner.)*

Good-night!
To each weary, toil-worn wight;
 And the busy fingers, bending
 Over work that seems unending,
Toil no more till morning light:
  Good-night!

Go to rest!
Close the eyes with slumber pressed;
 In the streets the silence, growing,
 Wakes but to the watch-horn blowing.
Night makes only one request:
  Go to rest!

Slumber sweet!
Blessèd dreams each dreamer greet:
 He whom love has kept from sleeping,
 In sweet dreams, now o'er him creeping,
May he his belovèd meet.
  Slumber sweet!

So, good-night!
Slumber on till morning light;
 Slumber till the new to-morrow
 Comes and brings its own new sorrow:
We are in the Father's sight:
  Slumber on!   Good-night!

# BEFORE THE SLEEPING STATUE OF THE QUEEN LOUISA.

*(From the German of Theodor Körner.)*

How soft thy sleep ! The tranquil features seem
To breathe again thy life's fair dreams e'en now;
'T is Slumber droops his wings around thy brow,
And sacred Peace hath veiled the eye's pure beam.
So slumber on till, O my country ! thou —
While beacon smoke from every hill doth stream,
And the long-rusted swords, impatient, gleam —
Shalt raise to heaven the patriot's holy vow.
Down, down through night and death, God's way
        may lie ;
Yet this must be our hope, our battle-cry :
Our children's children shall as freemen die !
When Freedom's morning, bloody-red, shall break,
Then, for thy bleeding, praying country's sake,
Then, German wife, our guardian angel, wake !

---

# A POET'S SOLACE.

*(From the German of Justinus Kerner.)*

WHEN I am dead, no eye of love
    May drop a tear upon my grave;
Yet weeping flowers shall bloom above,
    And sighing branches o'er me wave.

Though near the place where I shall lie,
  The passing traveller linger not,
Yet shall the quiet moon on high
  Look nightly down upon the spot.

In these green meadows where I rove,
  By man I may forgotten be;
Yet the blue sky and silent grove
  Forever shall remember me.

## THE GRAVE.

(*From the German of Von Salis-Seewis.*)

How silent and how crowded
  The dwellings of the dead!
Below, in darkness shrouded,
  An unknown land lies spread.

There sounds, when daylight closes,
  No nightingale's sweet tone,
And Friendship strews with roses
  The mossy mound alone.

In vain the bride, forsaken,
  May wring her hands and weep;
Nor orphans' wail may waken
  The dead ones from their sleep.

Yet nowhere else may mortals
　　Attain the wished repose,
And through the gloomy portals
　　Alone, man homeward goes.

The poor heart, tempest-driven,
　　There where all tempests cease,
Finds home at length, and heaven,
　　And everlasting peace.

———◆◇◆———

# VENICE.

*(From the German of Platen.)*

VENICE, calm shadow of her elder day,
　　Still, in the land of dreams, lives fresh and fair;
　　Where frowned the proud Republic's Lion, there
His empty prison walls keep holiday.
The brazen steeds that, wet with briny spray,
　　On yonder church walls shake their streaming hair,
　　They are the same no longer! Ah, they wear
The bridle of the Corsican Conqueror's sway!
Where is the people gone, the kingly race
　　That reared these marble piles amid the waves,
Which e'en decay invests with added grace?
　　Not in the brows of yon degenerate slaves
Think thou the traits of their great sires to trace:
　　Go, read them, hewn in stone, on Doges' graves!

15

## THE GOOD COMRADE.

*(From the German of Uhland.)*

I HAD such a faithful comrade,
  Not a truer soul could be ;
When the trumpet called to battle,
And the drum with roll and rattle,
  He still kept step with me.

A musket-ball came flying —
  Is it meant for me or thee ?
The fatal shot came speeding,
At my feet it laid him bleeding, —
  A bleeding piece of me.

He lifted his hand to greet me —
  I was busy loading then :
I cannot give my hand now —
Farewell — in heaven's bright land now,
  Thou bravest, best of men !

## PURITY OF LIFE.

*(From the German.)*

LIKE the traveller's path o'er mountain snow,
Be the path in which through life I go.
Oh, blessèd thought —
To mark the track, but stain it not !

## UHLAND'S LAST LINES.

*(From the German of Uhland.)*

AT midnight, on a wide and trackless sea,
When all the lights on shipboard are gone out,
And even in heaven there nowhere shines a star,
A little lamp burns dimly on the deck,
Its wick, protected from the violent winds,
Keeping the needle in the steersman's view,
That points him out unerringly his path;
So, if we guard it, we, in each dark pass,
Have a still light for guide, burning within the breast.

## SPRING REST.

*(From the German of Uhland.)*

LAY me not in the gloomy ground,
Not underneath the green grave-mound!
But, oh, if buried I must be,
Down in the deep grass bury me!

In grass and flowers I fain would lie,
With a low flute-tone wailing by,
And the bright spring-clouds overhead
Sailing along, — there make my bed.

## ON THE DEATH OF A COUNTRY PASTOR.

*(From the German of Uhland.[1])*

If to departed spirits Heaven e'er grants
Leave to revisit these their earthly haunts,
Not in the moony night wilt thou return,
When sorrow only wakes to weep and yearn;
No! when a summer morning greets the view,
When not a cloud-speck stains th' expanse of blue,
When high the golden harvest rears its head,
All intertwined with flowers of blue and red,
Then wilt thou through the fields walk as erewhile,
And greet the reapers with a pleasant smile.

---

[1] Bleibt abgeschiednen Geistern die Gewalt,
Zu kehren nach dem ird'schen Aufenthalt,
So kehrest du nicht in der Mondennacht,
Wann nur die Sehnsucht und die Schwermuth wacht;
Nein, wann ein Sommermorgen niedersteigt,
Wo sich im weiten Blau kein Woelkchen zeigt,
Wo hoch und golden sich die Ernte hebt,
Mit rothen, blauen Blumen hell durchwebt,
Dann wandelst du, wie einst, durch das Gefild
Und gruessest jeden Schnitter freundlich mild.

# The Romantic Tradition in American Literature

An Arno Press Collection

Alcott, A. Bronson, editor. **Conversations with Children on the Gospels.** Boston, 1836/1837. Two volumes in one.

Bartol, C[yrus] A. **Discourses on the Christian Spirit and Life.** 2nd edition. Boston, 1850.

Boker, George H[enry]. **Poems of the War.** Boston, 1864.

Brooks, Charles T. **Poems, Original and Translated.** Selected and edited by W. P. Andrews. Boston, 1885.

Brownell, Henry Howard. **War-Lyrics** and Other Poems. Boston, 1866.

Brownson, O[restes] A. **Essays and Reviews Chiefly on Theology, Politics, and Socialism.** New York, 1852.

Channing, [William] Ellery (The Younger). **Poems.** Boston, 1843.

Channing, [William] Ellery (The Younger). **Poems of Sixty-Five Years.** Edited by F. B. Sanborn. Philadelphia and Concord, 1902.

Chivers, Thomas Holley. **Eonchs of Ruby:** A Gift of Love. New York, 1851.

Chivers, Thomas Holley. **Virginalia;** or, Songs of My Summer Nights. (Reprinted from *Research Classics,* No. 2, 1942). Philadelphia, 1853.

Cooke, Philip Pendleton. **Froissart Ballads,** and Other Poems. Philadelphia, 1847.

Cranch, Christopher Pearse. **The Bird and the Bell,** with Other Poems. Boston, 1875.

[Dall], Caroline W. Healey, editor. **Margaret and Her Friends.** Boston, 1895.

[D'Arusmont], Frances Wright. **A Few Days in Athens.** Boston, 1850.

Everett, Edward. **Orations and Speeches,** on Various Occasions. Boston, 1836.

Holland, J[osiah] G[ilbert]. **The Marble Prophecy,** and Other Poems. New York, 1872.

Huntington, William Reed. **Sonnets and a Dream.** Jamaica, N. Y., 1899.

Jackson, Helen [Hunt]. **Poems.** Boston, 1892.

Miller, Joaquin (Cincinnatus Hiner Miller). **The Complete Poetical Works of Joaquin Miller.** San Francisco, 1897.

Parker, Theodore. **A Discourse of Matters Pertaining to Religion.** Boston, 1842.

Pinkney, Edward C. **Poems.** Baltimore, 1838.

Reed, Sampson. **Observations on the Growth of the Mind.** *Including,* **Genius** (Reprinted from *Aesthetic Papers,* Boston, 1849). 5th edition. Boston, 1859.

Sill, Edward Rowland. **The Poetical Works of Edward Rowland Sill.** Boston and New York, 1906.

Simms, William Gilmore. **Poems:** Descriptive, Dramatic, Legendary and Contemplative. New York, 1853. Two volumes in one.

Simms, William Gilmore, editor. **War Poetry of the South.** New York, 1866.

Stickney, Trumbull. **The Poems of Trumbull Stickney.** Boston and New York, 1905.

Timrod, Henry. **The Poems of Henry Timrod.** Edited by Paul H. Hayne. New York, 1873.

Trowbridge, John Townsend. **The Poetical Works of John Townsend Trowbridge.** Boston and New York, 1903.

Very, Jones. **Essays and Poems.** [Edited by R. W. Emerson]. Boston, 1839.

Very, Jones. **Poems and Essays.** Boston and New York, 1886.

White, Richard Grant, editor. **Poetry:** Lyrical, Narrative, and Satirical of the Civil War. New York, 1866.

Wilde, Richard Henry. **Hesperia:** A Poem. Edited by His Son (William Wilde). Boston, 1867.

Willis, Nathaniel Parker. **The Poems, Sacred, Passionate, and Humorous, of Nathaniel Parker Willis.** New York, 1868.